Andy Murray is the British No.1 and reigning Wimbledon and Olympic Men's Singles Champion.

From winning his first tournament as an under-10 junior at the Dunblane Sports Club, to his first junior major at the US Open, it became apparent very early that Andy was destined for the top.

After turning pro in 2005, Andy won his first ATP title, the SAP open in San Jose, a year later. Fast forward two years and seven more tour titles, he reached his first Grand Slam final, the 2008 US Open.

In 2012, having lost in three subsequent Grand Slam final appearances, Andy became the US Open Champion. This was hot on the heels of an illustrious Gold Medal victory at Wimbledon during the London 2012 Olympics.

Andy then ended years of heartbreak on the same turf just a year later by becoming the first Brit in 77 years to win the highly coveted Men's Singles title at the Wimbledon Championships.

On Sunday December 15th, Andy was voted the BBC Sports Personality of the Year for 2013.

ANDY MURRAY

SEVENTY-SEVEN

MY ROAD TO WIMBLEDON GLORY

headline

First published in 2013
by HEADLINE PUBLISHING GROUP

First published in paperback in 2014
by HEADLINE PUBLISHING GROUP

1

Cataloguing in Publication Data is available from the British Library

ISBN 978 0 7553 6597 5

Typeset by Palimpsest Book Production Ltd, Falkirk, Stirlingshire
Designed by James Edgar at Post98design.co.uk

Printed and bound in Great Britain by
Clays Ltd, St Ives plc

Headline's policy is to use papers that are natural, renewable and recyclable products and
made from wood grown in sustainable forests. The logging and manufacturing processes
are expected to conform to the environmental regulations of the country of origin.

I'd like to dedicate this book to Kim, my family, friends and tennis team (both past and present), and not forgetting Maggie and Rusty. Without all their love and support, the last year or so wouldn't have been possible.

The book is also for everyone who has supported me throughout my career, which includes my loyal sponsors: there are too many names to mention here but you know who you are.

I would like to thank everyone who has ever helped me, both on and off the court. The last 16 months have been amazing and I hope I was able to make you all proud. Here's to the future.

Thanks also to the guys at Headline and Neil Harman for putting the book together. I hope everyone enjoys the read.

Andy Murray,
October 2013

Contents

CHAPTER 1

I looked down at my left hand. For the first time I could remember in the middle of a tennis match, it was shaking. Shaking pretty violently.

I was in the midst of what would become the single game that would change everything in my life.

I had gone to collect the balls to serve. It was the first deuce of what would be four at 5-4 in the third set of the Wimbledon final. I had had three match points already, three chances to win the Men's Singles title, and Novak Djokovic, the world number one and a great champion, had so far resisted each time.

You never know how your body might respond

in these circumstances, but I had never had a reaction like that before. I suppose it showed how much it meant, but it was something that had caught me by surprise.

The week before Wimbledon I had endured my usual bout of mouth ulcers. They come on the Tuesday or the Wednesday before the Championships every year, the sign that although I try to block out all that the tournament means to me and to everyone else in the country, my body will respond to the pressure in a way I can't control. The ulcers tend to have disappeared by the time the event comes around, but they are a painful reminder of the time of year.

Players respond to these ultra-nervous moments in different ways. Some feel it in their head, a kind of excessive pounding, I imagine, which makes them want to rush the points, to try to get them over as quickly as possible, take risks. Some probably feel it in their arms, which stiffen up and make effective serving and the free-flowing ground strokes very difficult. It tends to get to me in the legs. They start to feel heavy, almost as if they have swollen, grown bigger, so I can't move as well as I would like.

But here we were at deuce, on Centre Court, on a really warm day, hotter than it had been for months. Having been three times within a solitary point of the title I had craved for so long, the gulf I had to bridge had now been extended to two points. That is when the shaking began.

A few minutes before, when I had sat down in my chair knowing that I was about to serve for the title, I really felt OK, like at the US Open the previous year. There was no sense of 'What do I do now?' or 'How can I handle this?' I had it in my mind that I would inevitably feel worse and be incredibly nervous: I don't know why, but I didn't actually feel that at all. I put the ice towel across my shoulders and the only thought I recall is that I wanted to ensure I got the first serve in, to make my opponent play. Those first points really do settle you down, especially on this surface, because you naturally think you will get at least one free point per service game on grass.

I had a sense of the crowd getting extremely excited: they were calling my name, I think, but I didn't hear it clearly enough to catch what they were saying. It was so noisy, I think I missed chair umpire Mohamed Lahyani's call of 'Time'. I walked back to the roller end and prepared to do what I had to do.

Of course, I knew I had this service game for the title. In the past, when I had put myself in this position, in the other Grand Slam tournaments, I felt the same way each time: they were all so important to me. In my head, I had built up those key moments so much that when they came they weren't actually as bad as I had imagined them to be. This is what I had been doing my whole life, the moments I have been training myself for. Yes, there were still nerves there, but I genuinely wasn't nervous in the Arthur Ashe Stadium against Novak in the US Open final in 2012 because I had two breaks in the fifth set, I had the wind with me and I knew he was going to have to produce something very special to come back.

At Wimbledon, though you have considered this precise moment on the practice court, it really is not that easy to visualise yourself in the position I found myself. You can tell yourself that you're serving for Wimbledon, but what happens if you miss the serve? Practice and reality simply don't add up when you build the scenario in your head. I can tell you that thinking about it and the reality of being out there and doing it are two completely different experiences. And having pictured where I wanted to hit that first serve, I actually missed it by quite a long way. On the second serve, Novak skipped around to hit a forehand to my forehand corner, to which I hit a forehand and he missed a backhand, long. I took a deep breath there. *15–love.*

I missed my first serve on the next point, too, into the net. He played a deep return on my second serve, we rallied briefly, he tried a drop shot from behind the baseline and I scampered up the court and put a forehand away from on top of the net. *30–love.*

I knew my next serve would be vital. I struck a big serve down the middle and Novak sent his backhand return long. *40–love. Championship point.*

Three chances for me to end it.

The crowd was shushing each other now. There were a couple of late shouts and I had to stop my serve as I was getting into the motion.

I hit a 131-mph serve out wide. Novak responded with a sliced backhand return, then another shot pretty close to the baseline. I scooped it up and he came into the net. Off the second of his volleys, I attempted a passing shot but he read it well. He played another couple of volleys, making outrageous 'gets' at the net, almost as a desperation tactic, but it forced me to scramble the ball back and he was able to play a winning forehand volley into the open court. *40–15.*

On the second Championship point, I narrowly

missed my first serve and he attacked my second, nailing a backhand return. *40–30.*

On the third, I missed the first serve once more. It flew long but there were some shouts from the crowd and I thought I would challenge. Novak's expression suggested I was completely wrong, but you never know. Not this time: it was six inches over the line.

The next rally was tight. I thought I had a back-hand opening down the line but unfortunately I missed it by an inch or so. *Deuce.* It was then, as I beckoned the ball boy to hand me a towel, that I saw that my left hand was shaking.

Somehow, I hit a good serve and Novak got in a superb return at full stretch. Again I had an oppor-tunity on the forehand: I went down the line and if I had gone back behind him I would have won the point after such a good serve but he was 'picking it' in those few points. If I had hit a couple the other way, I would have won the match earlier, but Novak guessed right. When I ran around a forehand, I missed it into the tape. *Advantage Djokovic.*

I have seen the replays of that game and at that moment the cameras focused in on my mum. She was saying, 'You're all right', but she wasn't thinking that. I just know it. For me it is so hard to watch that because I know my mum better than anyone and you can see what she is really thinking, you can see the stress of it all and how much she wants me to do well. It's not pleasant to put any of your family through that. I didn't like watching it back at all, seeing loved ones so nervous and so pent up.

At that point in the match I wasn't looking up to anyone at all. Normally I looked up to the box frequently, but in those circumstances – from 40-15 until the end of the match – I didn't glance up at my party because sometimes their faces and actions can affect how I am feeling. I needed to do this all on my own, to let what was going to happen happen and concentrate fully.

I have always loved the scoring in tennis: one moment you are certain you are going to win a match, then four points later you are right up against it and you realise anything can happen.

It's hard to describe accurately the pressure and nerves I was experiencing at that moment because I sensed that if I lost this point it might all be over, the opportunity completely gone. I was thinking that this could be the only chance I ever have, so it was unbelievably hard not to allow myself to think ahead, to think how it might feel having to play those points that were yet to come.

Yes, it was only a tennis match, but it was the most important one of my career, a match for which I have been training since I was 15: ten years of my life, training intensively to get into this position. There's such a huge amount of hard work resting on a couple of points, and I was close to blowing it. Yes, it was hard. That is why half an hour after leaving the court, I felt dead, a totally spent force.

I was a break point down, but I nailed a lovely serve down the middle, forcing Novak to miss his forehand return. *Deuce.*

I screamed 'C'mon' to myself. I needed the crowd at this point. I pumped my fist. It was a great free point, and they don't come very often against Novak. I had to keep on believing and hope that the pressures wouldn't get to me entirely. I didn't think they would, even after those shakes.

The next rally was incredibly intense, one of the best of the match. Novak was striking out for all he was worth, my defences were sound from around the baseline. I might have hit one backhand a touch short and he came in, got a half-volley on the ball, and it touched the top of the net before landing softly on my side. What can you do but shake your head and get on with it? *Advantage Djokovic.*

Break point down again, I missed my first serve but floated in a decent second one which he attacked on the backhand. This turned into another incredibly tough rally, more than 20 strokes. I thought Novak may have stopped at one stage, when I hit a backhand that was very close to going out. He nudged the ball back and I tried to get up to it and give it enough spin to bring it back down in time, because when the ball stays that low it needs a certain amount of height to get it over the net: bringing it down still within the court is tough, especially at the end of a rally of that intensity. But it was a winner. *Deuce.*

On that deuce, he played a short ball and I was drawn forward and thought I'd drop-shot him, take him by surprise, but he was really quick onto it and feathered a beautiful forehand dink cross-court. I felt my legs go heavy. That tended to be my pressure sign, but I simply had to get myself up for the next point. *Advantage Djokovic.*

I hit a decent serve, Novak played a good return but it was short enough for me to take on the fore-hand up the line and, with him stretching to get his backhand back in play, I was able to move forward and cut the ball off at the net with a backhand volley. *Deuce.*

I spoke to Ivan Lendl, my coach at the time, after the tournament about what I had done well or not so well during my Wimbledon fortnight. I told him I thought I could have done a better job of dictating the points earlier in the match. But the one thing I did well was when I was faced with break points, I forced the issue and made the point happen.

I had been practising for 18 months to make sure I went for those shots. I responded well in the biggest pressure moment there can be. It shows that if you practise something enough, it can become second nature. That is what you train for, so that even when you are nervous your body does respond well to the demands placed on it. I came up with a big forehand. It was all good. I think I broke my 'don't look up' concentration then, but I just wanted to show that everything was good. My mind was still fresh.

The next rally was pretty intense too. Once more I missed my first serve, which didn't help, and the second serve was only 80mph so we engaged again from the back of the court, slices and more aggressive shots mixed in. I remember Novak playing a really aggressive forehand deep into my forehand corner. I managed to respond and his attacking forehand down the line meant I could only throw up a defensive lob. If Novak is susceptible to anything, it is under the high ball and he didn't get everything on his overhead. This time I guessed right, stayed in the backhand corner and managed to get a good two-hander cross-court. He still got a racket on it, played a touch-volley but I had anticipated it and cracked a forehand that he could do nothing with. *Advantage Murray.*

Championship point. My fourth of the match.

You just do the routine things in that moment: towel yourself down, look for the two best balls, and get ready. But your heart is pounding in your chest that much faster, the adrenalin takes over. I had a fourth chance. My serve could not have been better but Novak got that one back as well, hanging out a racket. I had to quickly get my feet into a position where I could play an off-forehand which wasn't one of my best. He took aim with a backhand down the line . . . and netted it.

● ● ●

Straight after winning the US Open final last year, I was totally shocked. You could see that I could barely believe what I'd achieved by the way I reacted, hands over mouth, looking up to my box almost with a vacant expression.

But on Centre Court, I understood the manner of the win. I let go of my racket, flicked off my hat. I wanted to celebrate with everyone.

At the US Open, as big as the tournament is, and even though it was my first Slam, I didn't feel the same sense of expectation on my shoulders. New York felt like an individual accomplishment, but at Wimbledon it was different because it had been so many years since the last British winner of the Men's Singles, and the home crowd were so supportive and so expectant.

Wimbledon was for everyone. It was for my team, the media, the crowd, the huge TV audience.

I had never planned what I would do when I won Wimbledon, and my reaction would suggest that I didn't have a clue what I was doing.

I turned towards the BBC commentary box where I knew Tim Henman and the rest of the media guys were. I hugged Novak (if he said anything to me, I'm sorry but I can't remember what it was). I went down on my knees, taking big, deep, incredibly elated breaths then went back to that corner of the court, high-fiving total strangers.

I really didn't know where I was walking: I was going wherever my feet were taking me. Nobody really knew where I was going. I didn't know where I was for a while, to be honest. It was spontaneous, totally spontaneous. That moment was chaotic. One big blur.

I hadn't heard the umpire read out the score, but I didn't need to. I knew what I had done. I was acutely aware of what I had achieved. I had won Wimbledon and my overwhelming sensation at that moment was that I wanted to share it with everyone there.

CHAPTER 2

As a general rule of thumb, my career has been one of steady progression. I believe that never getting too far ahead of myself has helped with that process a very great deal.

There was the occasional massive step – I seem to recall going from number 350 in the world rankings to inside the top 100 in next-to-no time – but as I reflect on things, I sense that it has been better for me to take things the way I have. It is only in the last few months, with victories in the Olympic Games, the US Open and then, of course, at Wimbledon, that events have taken on a very different and rather mind-numbing complexion.

Of course, we all want to succeed at everything

we do as quickly as we can. It's only natural. But in retrospect, the way I have gone about my career, one small step at a time, has been beneficial.

Thinking back to my first Grand Slam final, against Roger Federer at the 2008 US Open, I was very immature; both physically and in terms of my craft. It does seem an age ago, but it is only five years. I remember very little about that match except that it felt to me that it came around so quickly. I was pretty fortunate to get to the final. I defeated the Austrian Jürgen Melzer in the third round in five sets from two sets down, and then there was the semi-final against Rafael Nadal. I had never beaten him, despite five previous attempts. Though I didn't feel particularly stressed, the way the match unfolded – being switched from the Louis Armstrong to the Arthur Ashe Stadium because it wasn't possible to complete it in a single day due to rain – meant it took quite a bit out of me.

I was back on court 24 hours later to play Roger Federer. In truth, I wasn't really ready for the experience. I felt that it came around so fast, and the match itself went by really quickly (6-2, 7-5, 6-2 in an hour and 51 minutes). I don't think I learned anything from the experience that would help me in future matches.

Maybe I was simply overwhelmed. Roger had

played so many major finals before, and given the difference in experience it was pretty much a mismatch. I wasn't nervous the night before, just excited. Maybe that was because I didn't have enough expectation of myself to win the match.

That's what I mean about the gradual progress that I have made throughout my career, with my results, my performances. To have beaten Rafa and Roger in consecutive matches like those at that stage would have been a massive jump. But as things have transpired, it has been about reaching landmarks such as my first final at the US Open (and losing), my first final in Australia (and losing), my first French Open semi-final (and losing), and my first final at Wimbledon (and yes, you guessed it, losing).

All of these steps along the road, and others such as beating Rafa, beating Novak, beating Roger for the first time (huge moments in their own way): nothing I have done has come straight away. Beating Rafa in New York in 2008 at the time may not have seemed to be of major relevance, because I went on to lose the final, but it was another crucial little step in the right direction.

● ● ●

The only thing about my progress that could be considered really dramatic was when I broke into the top 100. I always wanted to get there. In basic terms, that was my initial target as a professional player. When I moved over to Spain to the Academia Sánchez-Casal, I had in the back of my head I would only consider myself a success if I could climb the ladder and get my ranking down to two figures.

At my first Wimbledon (2005), I played well and reached the third round where I led David Nalbandian of Argentina by two sets to love, but I couldn't quite sustain that level. I remember working with coach Mark Petchey ('Petch') for ten weeks in a row and I rode that momentum from Wimbledon, the grass-court season, all the way through into the US Open. I felt that I was going to make a real career of this, that I was on my way.

I would never play nine or ten weeks in a row now, but as an 18-year-old, playing all the time was what I wanted to do. I have been asked if I have been goal-orientated or process-orientated during my career, but at that time I just wanted to get into the top 100, and if that meant playing ten weeks in a row I didn't care.

Within those ten weeks, I did make it to where

I wanted to be. But, in time, I started to understand that to reach even more ambitious goals was going to be a much slower process. Those achievements do not come overnight.

It is when you have to deal with the expectations of others – and I think I have had my fair share of carrying that burden – that you come to realise how significant and imperative a strong support team becomes. Back then, Petch was really protective of me. We didn't work together for that long, but in that period, and still today, he has been on my side. He sees it from my point of view, because he knows who I am and that I did what I needed to do to become this player. I lived with him. I spent plenty of time with his kids when I was working with him. It is difficult to say that he treated me like a son because we weren't that far apart in age, but I felt that was close to the kind of relationship I had with him.

I know how important he was in my career because I had just left Spain and it was obviously going to be a critical phase of my journey. Petch had his job with Sky Sports and it was a big wrench for him, having a young family, to leave South Africa to come out and support me. But he is one of the guys who really believed in me when I was in my mid-teens. From the very first time he saw me play, he always backed me, and when he was in charge of the men's game at the LTA, he was always right behind me.

I love being around him; we had great fun together, I enjoyed travelling with him and I was set with him before I had reached 18. Tim Henman and Greg Rusedski were at the top of the British game but they weren't playing the same tournaments as me. Petch and I were striking out into unchartered waters, on our own.

I needed someone who could discipline me, look after me, but also care about me. Petch was trying to protect me from some of the mercenary people who surround professional tennis tournaments; who might have an interest in backing you financially, or might try to muscle in on any future success. You need people beside you who are standing up for your interests.

It is not only tennis that attracts unscrupulous people trying to take advantage. One of the things I hate about sport is that there are so many people trying to profit from young kids who are just trying to play.

I have had to make many choices in my life as a professional to try to ensure I am in the best possible position to allow myself to play to my maximum on court. In every respect, I am pleased with those choices. They have helped shape me and, in some way, I hope they have shaped for the better the lives of those who have been on this journey with me. I owe numerous people a debt of gratitude for all they have done.

As far as my line-up of front-line coaches is concerned, from Mark Petchey, to Brad Gilbert, to Miles Maclagan, to Àlex Corretja, and to Ivan Lendl, with Dani Vallverdu as a constant throughout so much of that time – I have had (and almost as importantly, still have) great relationships with all of them. I would go out to dinner with every single one of them now. That is such a good feeling to have. When I finish playing it will be so important to me that all of the people I've worked with will remain friends with me; that they have enjoyed being a part of my life.

When I listen to them on TV, Petch and Brad are enormously supportive. That comes from having been around me, from understanding me, knowing me, having to deal with my good and not-so-good, for as long as they have. That is enormously gratifying. They are not only trying to see it from my side: they are objective, they have strong opinions, and they make great sense. But they are also very protective towards me, and that is very touching.

● ● ●

When it comes to my management companies, I have moved a couple of times. These transitions have always been undertaken with the best of intentions, in the interests of my career and development.

I first signed with Octagon when I was 13 years old. It was not my decision – that is the way these things get done. Don't get me wrong, the folk at Octagon are really good people and I get on with them still, but I don't like the side of the sports business that sees firms signing kids at 13 years old.

Of course, these operations have the funds to back you if you need to go and train abroad (as happened in my case), because tennis is an expensive sport and you can see why parents might go for that. But I don't think it is ideal. I'm not saying every single agent and management company is taking advantage, but I've been around now long enough to know there are people out there I wouldn't trust. When I am done playing this game, I could see myself working to help younger players make the right sort of decisions. For me, at that tender age you want to be able to enjoy your tennis, to get the coaching and facilities you require without all the extra pressure being put on you, and your parents, from management companies.

I made my next move when I was 18. It was partly my decision but my family was also very involved, because even at that age, you really don't have the life experience to make such important judgments. You are putting a lot of trust in people, and you don't know how much they care about you, or how much they want success for you. You make choices based on instinct, and I went with a smaller company that would be able to give me a little more of their time.

I joined Ace Group and was managed by Patricio Apey, from whom I learned an awful lot. It was a crucial time in my career. Brad Gilbert came in as my coach, and there seemed to be so much I wanted to do.

But I suffered my worst-ever injury on my 20th birthday, just when I thought I was on the cusp of doing so well. It was a setback I really learned from. That wrist injury in Hamburg in May 2007 was a defining one. I was worried not only about how it might affect me in the short term but in the long term as well. I remember the rumours suggesting I wouldn't play again, but I never have been a quitter.

There was conflicting advice as to whether I could play Wimbledon that year but I knew in my heart of hearts that it wouldn't work. The distress was caused not by making the decision – it was almost never an option in my opinion, although Brad thought I might have been able to play – but by the general disappointment at having to miss The Championships. I didn't play for over two months after the initial injury but even then I didn't feel I was ready.

It was around this time I realised that Brad and I were not seeing things the same way. I felt he didn't listen enough to what I was trying to say and he probably felt I was being too negative. We parted company later that year. Not so long after that, I changed management companies again.

I first met Simon Fuller, the head of XIX Entertainment, in 2008, essentially because of my brother Jamie and my mum. We all sat down to talk about new things and what direction we should all

take. I know that if I met with four different management companies they would pretty much say exactly
the same thing in their presentations, but Simon was
very different. He thought outside the box, and I
found his approach refreshing. It wasn't so much what
he said about me but what he said about the people
who he had worked with before.

Simon was involved when the former Liverpool
midfielder Steve McManaman went to Real Madrid.
He recommended that Steve should let his contract
with Liverpool expire, and then sign for Real. That
way, Real would not have to pay a transfer fee and,
in turn, they could then pay Steve a higher salary.

McManaman was entitled to let his contract run
out – and usually football agents want their players
to go to as many clubs as possible because they get
a fee. Simon wasn't necessarily looking at it like that
because he and Steve were friends rather than simply
business acquaintances.

I was still concerned about XIX's lack of in-house
tennis expertise. That instinct proved to be right, and
after a while I felt we had to bring in a couple of
people with intimate knowledge of the tennis business
to work for me.

This sport can be so complicated; unless you are

immersed in it all the time it is very hard to understand fully. There were offers for me to move – attractive ones – but I felt a bond with Simon and I told him that I wanted different people to work with me. I was really pleased when Ugo Colombini, an Italian agent I have known since I was playing the European junior circuit as a 12-year-old, came into the team. I've found having him around to be extremely beneficial.

After I lost the Australian Open final to Novak in 2011, I remember being startled when one of the agents who was with CAA (Creative Artists Agency), a firm with a strong association with Simon Fuller, was sitting in the Djokovic box. When I came back into the locker room, the agent was also drinking champagne out of the winner's trophy. This is the sort of situation that can arise sometimes, and I felt it was regrettable.

I have said it many times but it bears repetition: you need to make sure you surround yourself with the right people. Now I have the right people in place.

It is imperative that I get to know those who work with me, and that they really understand me. I know that there have been times when it has seemed as if I did not want to do the kind of corporate schmoozing that is part-and-parcel of high-level professional sport.

If someone from a management company wanted to come and see me train for a month in Miami, not just for one day, and I saw that they were really keen to get to know what I did and how committed to my profession I am, then they would realise that I am not the kind of guy who wants to go straight from the court, have a shower and then do a five-hour photo shoot before flying to LA to be a guest on an awards show, or to go home to London for something else and then come back and pick up training the next day. There are certain times of year I don't want to do anything but train, and there are times of the year when I'm more than happy to do other things, so long as it fits.

My training is vitally important to me. It's unfair on those you work with if they are not given an opportunity to do their jobs properly. Let's say one of my fitness trainers wants me to train hard for five days a week for three weeks, and then have a specific number of days off. If halfway through that period I jet off all over the world doing photo shoots, I'm not allowing them to do what they are here to do.

I'm happy to do some stuff: I've been on *The Jonathan Ross Show,* appeared in *A League of Their Own* and *World Cup Live,* posed for *GQ.* Yes, I have done some commercial stuff, but much less than other players might choose to do. I want to make sure I do the right things and prepare properly, rather than dancing off somewhere to make extra money.

When I sat down with the guys after Wimbledon this year my feeling was to be patient, not just agree to a deal with the first company that came along. I wanted to do things for the right reasons.

My team understand what I need, and which times of the year I'm really busy. If a company says they want me for eight hours in the week before Wimbledon, there is absolutely no chance of that happening. It's a balancing act to get all of your work done off the court so you can be as successful as you can be on the court: that is the priority. You fit the off-court work around the training.

A good example of my dedication to doing this right is that in the last three or four years, I have played only one exhibition match. I get offers all the time and I guess I would go somewhere sensible if I was able to be there for the whole week and it didn't interrupt my training. But I'm not going to fly one night to Brazil, one night to Mexico, one night to Canada and so on, because it would be impractical and highly disruptive. If exhibitions are scheduled properly, I'm happy to go. But tournament tennis has to be my priority, because that is my life.

● ● ●

Towards the end of 2011, I spoke to Darren Cahill, the Australian who worked as part of the Adidas team of coaches, and asked if he would consider leaving that role and coming to work for me full time. I have a tremendous regard for Darren's coaching abilities. He did wonderful things for Lleyton Hewitt and Andre Agassi – two players regarded for their work ethic and training structures – and I thought we would really fit well together.

I discovered – though I wasn't entirely surprised – that Darren was really happy at Adidas, and his commitments there and to his television career meant that going out on the road full time with one player was not an option for him.

Darren had helped me through a period in 2011 when I didn't have anyone other than Dani working with me on the coaching side. When I realised it wasn't going to happen with Darren, he said he would help me try to find the right person for the job.

Believe me, there were offers coming from every-where, from those wanting to help to those wanting to coach; from former top players to just about anyone you could think of. Some had absolutely no chance: random British coaches and ex-British players and commentators. Everyone was offering advice and saying how they could help.

I suppose I could have been flattered by all the offers, but I couldn't understand why some people came forward. There was absolutely no way they could help. Was it a matter of ego? Or were some watching me and thinking 'Yes it is so obvious what he needs'? The problem was, it wasn't obvious what I needed. Not everyone knows how to overcome losing in Grand Slam finals over and over again, or how to defeat some of the greatest players in the game. How many people know how to do that?

I was interested in Bob Brett, another Australian, who had coached Boris Becker and Goran Ivanišević and had been with Marin Čilić for quite some time, but he didn't offer his services. I wasn't really expecting him to call and say 'I am desperate to work with you' because people who are desperate don't tend to be the right people. Bob's credentials are impeccable. I really like him, but it wasn't to be.

With Darren as the conduit, the choice came down to two people: Roger Rasheed and Ivan Lendl. Roger had worked on the tour for a long time. We always got on well together. He had coached Hewitt and then Gaël Monfils, the Frenchman, and he had a great personality. I knew he would work me hard, that he had a great appreciation for the game. I enjoyed our talks. I thought it could be a good fit because I really, really like and respect him.

Darren came to Miami for a week or so during my training block to help me out on the practice court and he said he had set it up for me to meet Ivan. Darren, Dani and I drove up to Boca Raton for the meeting. I'm not sure I had spoken to Ivan directly about the role at this point. We met, we spoke, Ivan asked me about the other leading players: Roger Federer, Rafael Nadal and Novak Djokovic. He asked what I thought of their games, he told me his opinions.

Darren, Dani and I chatted a lot in the car on the way back to Miami. I thought more about it. I spoke to Roger Rasheed on the phone. He was willing to come over to Florida from his home in Australia to work with me on court. I pondered it some more. I spoke to Ivan on the phone and went back to Boca and practised with him on the court. From those two face-to-face encounters, I made up my mind.

I don't know how many people at the time thought that Ivan was the right person for me, because he had been away from tennis for a while, but I felt that there was something intriguing about his career and how it had played out. I liked the fact that people had found him difficult to appreciate and he wasn't at all about the fame: it was about the winning for him. And he was particularly unpretentious. The next time we met at some rubbish Italian restaurant in the middle of a strip mall next to a hairdressers just off Interstate 95 in Florida, and we agreed the deal. I have never made a better decision.

● ● ●

I decided to play in the Brisbane International for the first time in 2012. I had been at the Hopman Cup in Perth for the previous few years, a mixed event where I played with Laura Robson. It guaranteed you a set number of matches. Though the tournament was staged indoors, the outdoor conditions in Western Australia at that time of year were well suited to the kind of training I needed to do for the forthcoming Australian Open.

I was struggling with my right knee at the beginning of the Brisbane tournament; not the usual bipartite patella but a new injury just below the kneecap. Yet after the first few matches there – the first couple of which I had to pull out of the fire – I was beginning to feel better.

Ivan arrived on the Friday and I won the title on Sunday, dedicating it to 'Mr Lendl'. He hadn't even met all of the team at that point, so when we got to Melbourne he suggested we went out for a team dinner. I thought he might suggest Nobu, or a famous restaurant along those lines, but he arranged for us to meet in the food court at a casino. So that's what we did. The food was awful. Not that I cared. I like to eat nice food now I'm a little older, but to me it was refreshing that he didn't want us to be having a suit-and-tie stuffy dinner. I didn't know exactly what to expect from him, but it wasn't that.

It was a really good evening; we all bonded right away. I felt good about what was going to happen from the partnership but conscious, too, that some people were saying it was a lousy fit. Was it a risk? I suppose any of these coaching arrangements are a risk because you have no idea if you are going to click or not. Ivan told me that one of the reasons he was interested in coaching me was because he came to watch a couple of my practices at Nick Bollettieri's academy in Bradenton, Florida, when I was with Brad. He sat beside the court and at the end of my practice, we were introduced. He said I was really polite, very respectful of him, and it seemed like I worked hard.

I guess some people who don't know me may not think that would be the case, that I might not be particularly polite or well-mannered since my mouth on the court isn't always perfect. But it was something Ivan remarked on, and it has been one of the reasons he was interested in working with me. He is one of the best players ever to pick up a racket, and it was a challenge to take me on and to have major success as a coach. That's why he wanted to do it. I don't think Ivan viewed it as a major risk. He has tunnel vision; no negative thoughts.

I'm not saying that I'll go on to win eight Grand Slams like he has, but there are not many people in tennis who know what it is like to lose your first four Grand Slam finals – he is one of them, and so am I.

To be frank, at that stage of my career, I was

feeling like I was a loser: nothing more, nothing less. You wouldn't believe the abuse I would get walking down the street: people would swear and shout at me. If I went on Twitter, there was a ridiculous amount of abuse. I felt like a failure, even though I was one of the best in the world. I had won several tournaments; I should have been proud of what I'd achieved.

Ivan may not have had to endure quite so much. *Sports Illustrated* described him as 'The champion no one cares about' when he won the US Open in 1986. He has never given them an interview since.

It was not easy to cope with the belief that somehow I was a loser. My whole life I was the best at what I did. I was the best in my age group. I was the best in Britain; one of the best in Europe. I won the US Open juniors. I was thoroughly accustomed to winning major competitions. Yet I could win an event in Cincinnati and in the press conference immediately afterwards be asked: When are you going to win a Slam? Why haven't you won a Slam?

I know it's wrong, but at times my attitude towards an event like Cincinnati, a big event, actually became indifferent. People criticised me even when I won tournaments like this because all they were interested in was when I was going to win a Grand Slam.

Their preoccupation was contagious. I choked in the big matches. I beat Djokovic, Federer and Nadal in these 'lesser' tournaments, but it didn't mean anything. When I was winning these events but losing in the semi-finals of the Grand Slams, I was really heavily criticised.

If an article in the paper says my forehand was off in a particular game, I can take it. It's not a problem; that is part of the sport. But nobody deserves to be abused walking down the street.

Does it all go back to the 2006 World Cup, when I said something I meant to be an aside, a little joke? Has that one moment cursed me down the years? Maybe it has. It was the very last question I was asked during an interview. Who would I be supporting? 'Whoever England are playing' was my very clearly tongue-in-cheek reply. Some have never forgotten or forgiven, and it appears they never will. It seems to be the root cause for those who give the impression of disliking me with such fervour, whatever I do.

Rory McIlroy is going through something similar. Why should it be so difficult? Why are people so sensitive? Let Rory do what he wants to do, and be proud to do it. He is the nicest guy you could wish to meet. Why does his decision need to be politicised?

He is a sportsman, not a politician. In terms of who to represent in the Olympics, let him make the decision he wants to make, and support him.

Lee Westwood was ranked the number one golfer in the world, but because he hasn't won a major, he gets abused. I don't understand it. He seems like a really nice guy.

I think I am polite in my demeanour. My parents taught me that. I always say hello, please and thank you. I open doors for people. I think I have good manners.

Ivan Lendl knows better than me what it's like. He was disowned by his Czech homeland. He always told me not to read the press, not to listen. But I know he actually reads everything, what every journalist writes, what all the pundits say. He listens to all of it. He wanted me to ignore it.

● ● ●

When we got to Melbourne for the 2012 Australian Open, I felt really sharp. I said that I intended to show up and give 100 per cent on every point. I believe I did that. In the first five rounds I had dropped only a single set, the first of the tournament, to Ryan

Harrison of the United States, a young player who came out bombing and caught me being a little tentative. Once I got a foothold in the match, I was fine, and from that moment through to a semi-final date with Novak Djokovic, I played some really good tennis.

Then would come one of the most physically gruelling matches I had ever played. Novak is always a fierce competitor, but I established a lead of two sets to one and that should have been the moment to step it up. But I came out for the fourth set a little too relaxed and lost the set so quickly it went in a blur. I guess it was to be expected to suffer a comedown in the fourth set but I should have got off to a better start.

I was 5-2 down in the fifth set too, but fought back to 5-5 and had three break points. Novak got his first serve in every time – the hallmark of a champion – but I managed to get into a couple of rallies and I had my chances. At the end, I lost, yet I felt a lot better than I had done after previous big-match losses. Physically I knew I could still get stronger, for sure, but in comparison to how I had played the previous year, it was much, much better.

There had been some talk that I was generally

too passive in my play; that I didn't go for my shots enough. Against Novak, that wasn't the case. I probably made more mistakes than him, but I'm quite sure I hit more winners than he did. I was moving well and dictating many of the points, which was important.

I don't think I necessarily departed from my last couple of years in Australia with a fundamentally negative attitude: it felt more like temporary knocks to my confidence. I wasn't really down on myself or beating myself up. It was just the old question resurfacing – am I going to get there or not?

After the kinds of matches and experiences I've been through – I've lost a lot of tough matches – I've learnt to deal with them better. I bounced back well from most of the hard matches I lost in 2011: after the French, Wimbledon, and the US Open I did well. I hoped it would be the same again this time around.

The crowd in Australia has always been excellent to me and that's a considerable help. They were brilliant in the final in 2011, virtually on my side. I didn't feel like there was a huge difference between playing at Wimbledon and playing in Melbourne.

I'm not in the papers every day there. Everyone's more interested in Novak and Rafa, and Lleyton

Hewitt and Bernard Tomic, than they are in me. I've always preferred to be out of the spotlight rather than in it.

I reacted positively to that semi-final loss in 2012, realising I had fought as hard as I could. I was a different player with a different attitude. I recall saying that and believing it too. I was proud of the way I fought. Sometimes I come off and I'm disappointed that I've let myself down, but this time I didn't feel like that. There's a fine line between number one and number four and I felt I closed the gap that day. Everybody matures at different rates. I thought I was ready.

Tennis is such an individual sport. I love boxing: the fighter has his coach there after every round, the cuts man too; there is togetherness, they can give you advice on tactics. In tennis you play a five-hour match and you are out there entirely on your own. It is a hard sport mentally. When you get off the court after a defeat and you are sitting on your own, there's a wave that crashes over you: you start questioning everything about yourself. You question all the work you have done, everything about your game, your mentality. Everything.

In 2012, after the defeat to Novak, I had to

undertake a drug test. Ivan got the whole team to come and be with me for the test. They changed the rules that year, so after my urine test I had to sit down for 30 minutes before I was asked to give blood. There is a waiting room and all the team joined me in there.

When you come off after a match like that, you can feel an acute sense of isolation. To have friendly faces in the locker room, even if they aren't saying anything, is incredibly supportive. Ivan has been in that position, losing a marathon match. The guys distract you from thinking negatively. The odd smile can raise the spirits.

I thought Ivan dealt with that delicate situation so well. I hadn't won a Grand Slam: he knew it, and he knew what it meant. I sat down with him and Dani the next day and Ivan told me how proud he was of the way I fought. He said it was a great effort. Then he outlined the things I needed to work on if I was going to win these matches: nothing major, but factors that would make a difference. That was it.

I beat Novak in the semis in Dubai, but lost to Roger in the final. In Indian Wells I hadn't felt better for a long time. For a whole week I didn't miss a ball in practice. I told the press how good I was feeling and then went out and played terribly against

Guillermo García-López. It was a difficult one to explain. I went on to Miami and reached the final there, which goes to show that you can do all the right things in practice but performances in matches can sometimes be erratic. The skills in the game are so finely tuned, performance standards can fluctuate wildly. Maybe the wind changes, or the conditions are cooler. It is hard to explain: the way I was practising there was no way I thought I would lose in the first round in Indian Wells and then go on to reach the Miami final (where I lost 6-1, 7-6 to Novak).

We decided to practise on clay in Miami, but the club we usually use was being turned into a car park (such a shame), so we headed north to Boca Grove, a fantastic club, and had three days of solid clay court practice.

The clay-court season is the most demanding for me, and many other players. Some, like Rafa, adjust to the different surface like casually flicking a switch: he understands exactly what he needs to do. David Ferrer is another; the South Americans, too. But for me, it is the one surface on which I need to spend most time before I feel as if everything is working well. My movements have to change; the sliding becomes a vital part of the repertoire. It's clear how strong you need to be physically to compete all the time. Strength plays a key part, because the ball has to be struck up high. I love the clay, but it can be brutal as well.

Everybody was talking a lot about the courts in Monte Carlo that week in April. There are bad bounces of course, it's never perfect. If guys slide and dig up a bit of clay, those fragments can make life hard, but we all have to deal with the same thing. It does make it tougher to go out there and feel great all the time, to get excellent rhythm, to feel like your timing is perfect on the ball. That is something that's very important for me. That's how I play. I'm a ball striker. I rely on the quality of my returning.

During his career, Ivan played well on every surface and I knew he would help my clay court preparation, not just for the first tournament in Monte Carlo but for the six weeks on clay and the lead into the grass-court season. It may not have shown in the first or the second week, but it definitely helped after that. I had to pull out of Madrid because I was struggling a little with my back, and in Rome I wasn't at my best, losing to Richard Gasquet on the new court they had constructed for that year. Ivan gave Rome a miss because the place plays havoc with his allergies.

In 2012, they were particularly bad; he would have really suffered.

I suspect that quite a few people forget that I have been to the semi-finals of the French Open (2011), and had my chances against Rafa in all three sets. I guess it is regarded as the Grand Slam I have the least chance to win, and I suppose there is some truth to that.

My mind-set has changed, though, and I really want to be successful there. It is a matter of feeling good about all aspects of my game because without everything in good working order, I'm not going to be super-competitive. After my first-round match in 2012, I woke up feeling awful. My back was in spasm and I couldn't put any weight on my left leg. I discussed it with the guys and decided to play because I thought against Jarkko Nieminen, my Finnish opponent, I had a decent chance even if I wasn't 100 per cent, physically. I remember that during the first set I was really suffering, my back was bothering me and I needed treatment three times. I couldn't get much power on my serve. It was not a great situation, especially on Court Philippe Chatrier in front of a crowd who didn't really know how to react.

It is acutely lonely on court. Before the match

I was with the guys, talking about what I should do. But out on the court, especially during the first two sets, I wasn't looking up at anyone or engaging with anything they were saying at all. I was just so down about how I was feeling. I won through, though, in four sets.

The spasm was caused by the same chronic complaint I've suffered with my back for a long time. I finally shook it off and I won the match. Yes, my team had advised me to stop at the end of the first set but I decided to keep going, and obviously there was a dramatic turnaround.

From there, I defeated Santiago Giraldo in straight sets and Richard Gasquet, back on Philippe Chatrier, by exactly the same score as I had beaten Nieminen.

I remember being jeered onto the court by the French crowd at Roland Garros that day: that certainly got my competitive juices flowing, though I started as poorly as I had against Nieminen. This time, though, the back wasn't an issue and I won in four sets.

In the quarter-finals, my opponent was Spaniard David Ferrer, a ferocious competitor. I lost the first set, but it was indicative of how I was starting to figure out problems in my game and solve them, that I came back and won the second set, 7-6. Unfortunately that was when it started raining, and when I came out after the delay I struggled, and ended up losing the match 4-6, 7-6, 3-6, 2-6. For me, the change of conditions is one of the most compelling aspects of tennis – especially now that some of the stadiums have roofs. That change from outdoors to indoors means playing conditions can change very quickly. Also, the fact that there is no time limit on the match means the games are always exciting: a football team can score three goals and just defend that lead, but you can't do that in tennis. You are always in a position where you have to close things out, and the score-lines can change so quickly that you can go from being in a great position and three or four minutes later you're playing the most nerve-wracking point of your life.

Despite getting over my back trouble, I was still disappointed to go out against Ferrer. And I suffered a further setback in my next tournament, Queen's, when I lost my opening match to Nicolas Mahut, who was 65 in the world at the time.

I know that I can go out early in a tournament like Queen's but then bounce back. For example, in 2012 I would go out in straight sets at the Cincinnati Masters to unseeded Jérémy Chardy, but then went on to win the US Open. People might say it doesn't matter how I do in the smaller tournaments, but that's not the way I see it – I might know in my mind that I can still win the US Open after going out in the Cincinnati Masters, but that doesn't stop me wanting to win those smaller matches just as much. Aside from everything, the best preparation for any tournament is to win matches.

● ● ●

I was nicely prepared for Wimbledon in 2012. Yes, I had lost early at Queen's and played an exhibition match, but I had the feeling my game was where I wanted it to be. I had been asked a lot about my back, and it felt like some people didn't believe it was as bad as I was saying. At one point I actually showed some press guys the eight marks on my skin where the needles had gone in to help settle the problem.

My attitude had also come under scrutiny. I know that at times I had behaved in a way that hadn't helped me, but I've seen other players fall prey to their temper too, though the best ones can recover quickly. For example, I've seen Novak in matches where he has yelled and gone mental at his box, breaking rackets and getting really angry. Even in the 2011 Wimbledon final against Rafa he had almost tanked the third set but he came back and won.

I also recall David Nalbandian being disqualified in the final of Queen's in 2012. He kicked out in frustration at the advertising board in front of a linesman's wooden box and it splintered, injuring the linesman's leg. That was the end of Nalbandian that day.

Of course, ideally I'd not have any moments in matches where I get too negative, and it's something that I have tried to improve on during the last six years. But at the same time it had always been part of my personality to be emotional. I know if I went out on the court and didn't express any disappointment when things weren't going my way, I'd come off court and people would say, 'Andy, what was wrong with you today? You seemed flat on the court. You weren't expressing yourself.' I've tried various techniques, attempting to keep positive images in my head, but it's an ongoing process to deal with frustration on court.

I actually invited the press to come and spend a week with me in December 2012 when I was training so they could see all of the things I do off the court to prepare myself both mentally and physically. I think that benefitted everyone tremendously, because it opened their eyes to the lengths I take to prepare for games and it also gave me the chance to get to know them better.

There are times I express myself on court which might puzzle people. When I won my first-round match against Nikolay Davydenko at Wimbledon in 2012 I gestured with my two forefingers to the sky. It obviously intrigued many people because I got asked lots of questions about it. The real reason is that around that time I had a few friends and family who had various issues affecting them. I'm not particularly religious, but when I know people are going through a tough time, I'll think about them a lot – not necessarily to pray for them, but to reflect on the problems they're facing. It might be before I go to bed or when I wake up in the morning, but it is something I do quite a lot. So when I defeated Davydenko I knew that they would be watching and I wanted to let them know I was thinking of them, hence the gesture.

It may have been an easy victory for me in that first round, but I knew that facing Ivo Karlović would be much tougher, as he is one of the most stressful opponents to face. The reason I find it so hard to play him is that the way he plays dictates the atmosphere in the crowd. He is such a fast server – in fact he broke the record for the fastest serve in 2012 – that the points are so short. The crowd want to support you but as the games are so stop-start it's hard for them to engage in the match, and you can feel the tension from your side of the court because of the way the match is going. You may feel like you are playing the better tennis but Karlović neutralises what you are doing, so it is very tough.

I got broken in the very first game against him, which I wasn't really expecting, but I broke him straight back with a net cord and that relaxed me a little bit. I won the set 7-5, and despite dropping the next one 7-6, I went on to win the last two 6-2, 7-6.

My next opponent was another very tough one: Marcos Baghdatis. It was an interesting situation as his coach was Miles Maclagan, who I used to work with. Miles would have known my weaknesses so it was important for me not to try and second-guess how Marcos would play against me. I remember the boxer Floyd Mayweather saying it is very easy to win from outside the ring – working out which ways you can exploit your opponent – but if you're in the ring and they aren't behaving the way you've planned for, it can work against you.

The first two matches in the day had taken forever, so we didn't start until just before eight. I won the first set, but I was still struggling to figure out Marcos and he took the next set to level the match. Then the roof was closed, lending the court the atmosphere of a Saturday night at the theatre. I revel in this, but so does Marcos – he's a real showman and an incredible talent.

The grass was quite greasy and I slipped over three times. Twice the ball I pocketed for the second serve fell out, causing me to be warned and then lose a point.

The third set was a close-run thing, but I came out on top, winning 7–5. I then raced through the fourth set. Literally. There is an 11pm curfew at Wimbledon, and I didn't even sit down at the change of ends at 4–1. I had the balls in my hand to serve what proved to be the last game at one minute past eleven. The game took two minutes. 6–1. We were spared a Monday recall.

I went to bed feeling a bit frazzled. But my next opponent, Marin Čilić, must have felt even more knackered. He had defeated American Sam Querrey

17–15 in the fifth set, and I reckoned that even with a Sunday rest, he wasn't going to be in the greatest shape on Monday.

Our match was put on No.1 Court – and no, I didn't make a fuss about that, but the court does play a little different to Centre and takes a while to get used to. I won the first set 7–5 and I was 3–1 ahead in the second when the rains came and we knew we'd have to come back and finish the next day. At least we had started our match, many others were still kicking their heels.

I got the job done well on Tuesday, not taking too much time, and winning in three sets.

I was also pleased to discover afterwards that I was winning more points on my second serve than anyone else in the tournament. That was just as well because in the quarters, my opponent was David Ferrer, who had the second-best record. Ferrer is one of the strongest men on the tour and had, of course, just beaten me in the same stage at the French Open. He makes you work for every point. It knew it was going to be really tough, but I was delighted to be going back on Centre again.

I lost my serve first in both the first two sets and lost the first set on a tie-break when I had been in front. Ferrer served for the second set as well and I would not have relished trying to come back from two sets down, not against someone as tenacious and unforgiving as he is. He led 5–2 in the second set tie-break as well, so the match could have run away from me. I just kept saying to myself, 'Make him play, make him play'. He missed a couple and I seized the chance. I remember one particularly nice fore-hand winner to bring up set point and then he missed a cross-court backhand into the net. The third set was tight, but I won it 6–4 and then at 5–5 in the fourth we had to go off for more rain. It was only a brief interval before we were back out and heading into another tie-break. I played really well to take it 7–4.

At the end, I just felt a tremendous release of tension. I was into my fourth Wimbledon semi-final.

My opponent was Jo-Wilfried Tsonga, who offered another totally different challenge. No two shots are alike with Jo. He will thunder in an ace, he will come in, he'll throw himself around, he'll smash winners, he'll miss shots by a mile and smile. Jo seems to have boundless energy, then looks spent (people say I'm like that, too). And semi-final matches, with all that is at stake, are brutally tough. How do you seize control against someone who doesn't let you breathe?

As it turned out, I did grab the initiative. I went 2–0 up, serving as well as I had for quite some time. But Jo came back strongly, winning the third set 6–3. I got back on track at the start of the fourth, breaking serve to take a 3–1 lead. Then the skies darkened. I don't know whether that unsettled me, but I let my concentration dip and from being 3–1 up, it was suddenly 4–4.

I had a break point in the ninth game, but fell over trying to reach Jo's audacious drop shot. At 5–5, I went 15–40 down and was on a second serve at 30–40. Jo moved in and I thought he was bound to crunch a forehand winner but he missed it by several inches. I held for 6–5 and most people probably had a tie-break in mind but at 15–30, he threw himself at a volley and missed it into the net. I hit a beautiful forehand return on match point which caught the side-line. Jo challenged the call with a big beam on his face. We both knew the match was over. It had been more of a mental than a physical challenge and I'd come through.

● ● ●

Roger Federer had beaten Novak Djokovic in the first semi-final. If I was to become the champion I would have to beat the greatest grass court player of all time.

I was nervous. I needed to win this match. I needed to win a Slam. And I really thought I had a chance. I felt so different to how I did before my first Grand Slam final, against Roger in the 2008 US Open. This time I felt like I was in a comfortable, settled place. I knew what I had to do. Mentally, I was prepared to win. I felt that I was ready.

I started well, breaking him in the first game and again at 4–4 to be able to serve for the first set. I needed this set badly and I wasn't nervous serving for it. I felt as good as I could possibly have done. 6–4.

In the second set, I had a couple of break points that I vividly recall. On one, I hit a cross-court passing shot which he volleyed behind me. The next, I went full-blooded for a backhand winner down the line. I could have hit it down the middle of the court, and that might have happened in the past, but I decided to go for the winner. I just missed it. Roger took the set 7–5.

We went off for rain a couple of games into

the third set and they closed the roof. Roger came out more aggressive from there. His timing is so good: when there is no wind to disturb him, he strikes the ball superbly. I don't think I played any worse, it was just that he played a little better. He was in his element.

At 3–3, I led 40–0 and he played a really good drop shot which I fell trying to reach. That stunned me a little. I think he could see that in my eyes. He got it back to deuce and piled on the pressure. I had to save five break points, but couldn't save a sixth. He was ahead from that moment on, taking the set 6–3 and easing over the line 6–4 in the fourth.

I have seen loads of players crying in locker rooms after games, and heard stories about people breaking down. Normally you can get off the court pretty much straight away so you can do that in private. Not in major finals, though, and I knew when I was going up to be interviewed on court straight after the defeat to Roger it was going to be really hard.

When I went to speak, the crowd turned the volume up and I sensed they knew what I was feeling. They made so much noise I had to wait for them. Sue Barker started to ask a question, but I knew people hadn't heard, so I ended up taking the microphone from her and just tried to say what I was feeling.

There was no time to think about what to say. I hadn't pictured myself losing or worried about what I might say if I did. My mind was in turmoil and the words just came spilling out. In sport, the interviews are usually so choreographed, but this was totally spontaneous.

I was just pleased that in those few moments, people saw my true personality. I appreciate the support I get, I really do. It helps so much. In the past maybe I didn't have everyone behind me, but that summer was the first time I really felt like the crowd were saying, 'He is one of us'. They really, really wanted me to win, they understood me and how much it meant.

I apologised to Roger for reacting the way I did, but he said not to worry, it showed how much I cared. He is a great champion. I came away proud of what I had achieved. Although I was upset that I hadn't won, there was no second-guessing myself thinking, 'What if I had done that differently?' I had gone for my shots, but for a set and a half at the end of the match, he just played brilliantly.

In the locker room, Ivan said he was proud of me too, and that I'd be better next time. I believed him, but it didn't stop me having to endure one of the saddest nights of my life.

CHAPTER 3

The tears had dried a couple of days after the Wimbledon final. My spirits were high again and my girlfriend Kim and I decided we would take up the invitation to attend a screening of *Mock The Week*. I've watched the show for years. They've taken the p*** out of me plenty of times and I've loved it. I didn't think going there for a live showing was going to be so bad, because everyone had seen how much losing the Wimbledon final had meant to me. The attitude of the guys on the show was, 'We're not going to go too hard on him'. I got asked to go again after actually winning Wimbledon in 2013. The guys in the show joked that after I went on in 2012 all the titles have come – how could Ivan take all the credit?

When I played Wimbledon for the first time, it was different. When you're young, a bit precocious, you tend to say the first thing that comes into your head and it may or may not be appropriate. Ernests Gulbis, for example, does that now. I don't think what he says about the top players being dull is necessarily his real opinion – he says it for effect and it has worked as far as headlines are concerned.

When I was 18, I just responded to questions asked of me without giving the words a great deal of thought. If a stranger comes up to me now and starts asking questions, I'm not going to give the same answer as I might give my best friend. There is a fine balance between telling the truth and not telling all of your story. I try to focus on the parts that are relevant and leave the rest.

I do care what people think about me – find me someone who doesn't. I've had my fair share of criticism. I would like people to know exactly who I am. Perhaps when they see me in a TV interview, after a match, for instance, when I'm being quite thoughtful and controlled in what I say, they think that I'm this boring, dreary bloke. That isn't the case. If they saw me five minutes before or after the interview, and I was among friends, people I trust, they'd see a very different person.

I lost trust in the press around that late-teen period because I was doing many interviews and conferences and I didn't think I was being treated as fairly as I should have been. Consequently, I went from being very open and excitable to less open to rather closed off. That was a hard transition for me.

As an impressionable, self-conscious teenager, getting burned in the press as I did – constantly slated for the way I talked, my demeanour, the way I dressed. . . everything – it is hard to take. I just wanted to play tennis.

It was only when the tennis journalists started to understand that side of me and I got to know their job and their personalities a lot better, that a mutual understanding and respect developed. I can't recall the last time I had any problems with them and I know that every one of them wants me to do well. That may have always been the case, but when I came off court having lost and was getting asked negative questions all the time, I didn't appreciate that.

As a kid, my coach would tell me what I could improve on and it was usually a case of 'Don't worry, you are doing great'. My mum always said: 'It doesn't matter, so long as you are enjoying yourself'. That changes when you become a professional. It isn't about enjoying yourself any more, it's about winning.

I always wanted to win anyway. I was extremely competitive. When I lost matches in ATP Futures tournaments at 15, I'd be disappointed. The difference then was that I could call my mum and speak to my coach and they'd tell me it was no big deal. They just wanted me to be OK. That changed when I turned pro. The first people I saw when I came off court were the media and they do care whether you win or lose. It's very important to them, it dictates how they do their job, what they are going to ask, what they're going to write.

●　　●　　●

After the 2012 Wimbledon final, I hope people who didn't like me before might at least have understood me better and saw how much I care about tennis. I really want to do well, I really want to win, and not just for myself – I understand how important Wimbledon is for tennis in Britain.

After Wimbledon in 2012, I didn't feel I needed

to walk with my head down. I wasn't embarrassed that I cried on the court, I felt better for doing it. I went to certain events afterwards, like *Mock The Week*, where I got a standing ovation when the crowd was told I was there, and that would not necessarily have happened before. That match changed a lot for me.

Having the Olympics to look forward to just after Wimbledon helped me rebound strongly from the Federer loss, even if the few days afterwards were pretty unpleasant. It wasn't easy. I cried the whole way home and cried for hours more. I couldn't stop.

I had never reacted to a match like that in my life. Yes, I had been upset and disappointed before, but defeats were nothing new to me and I'd had my fair share of setbacks at critical moments in my career. I had cried a little bit on my own after a match, but never anything like this. At one stage I didn't think I'd ever stop.

Kim was there with me. She was upset because she had wanted me to win, but, as always, she just wanted me to feel happy more than anything else. This was something totally different to my normal post-defeat reaction, and she put up with all of that.

I went outside into the garden with the dogs, but I couldn't even find any comfort or consolation with them. I was in a bit of a state pretty much the whole night.

As upset as I was about losing the final, I was pleased that I'd really gone for it. I had lost in previous Grand Slam tournaments and felt I could have done so much better. I was angry with myself in those circumstances, but this time I was satisfied that I had done my absolute best and it just hadn't been enough.

Ivan told me that as well as being proud of how I had played at Wimbledon, he was impressed by how I'd handled everything that surrounded the tournament. He'd experienced pressure playing there himself, but I don't think he had experienced anything like this. When he was going out to dinner, people were coming up and asking what would happen, could I win and even he was getting bothered by it all. He said he couldn't possibly imagine what it was like for me.

Quite quickly I put the disappointment behind me and soon I wasn't thinking about Wimbledon, only the Olympics. And my practice for the Games was the best I can remember. I don't think I'd ever hit the ball better. It was great straight away whereas it normally takes a few days.

● ● ●

The Olympic Games particularly appeals to me because I have always loved team competitions. Since I was 12, I'd played lots of them – LTA summer and winter cups through all the age groups, and Davis Cup ties – and I knew that being part of a home Olympics would be a once-in-a-lifetime experience. That's not something you can say very often when you're only in your mid-twenties and have been playing at a top level for five or six years. Having my brother, Jamie, plus Colin Fleming and Ross Hutchins with me, guys I've known since I was ten, was only going to make a cool experience even better. I would play doubles with Jamie and mixed with Laura Robson.

There has been much debate about whether tennis should be an Olympic sport. To me, it comes down to how many quality players are in the field. When the best players skipped the Olympics, I could understand the argument against it being in the Games, but when I saw Roger winning a gold medal in the doubles with Stan Wawrinka in Beijing and how much that meant to him, with everything else he has achieved in his life, I just think it is right to have it. We get criticised if we don't play Davis Cup, and clearly there are some scheduling issues with that event that require some radical changes, but the Olympics is a terrific team competition. We love that it is for just one week, every four years and you don't get a second chance for another four years, if ever. I think that's one of the reasons why I responded so well to it after my Wimbledon disappointment.

What had happened in Beijing in 2008 only added to my sense of anticipation. I wanted to put that right. Beijing was one of the best experiences I'd ever had as an athlete. To be involved and part of the team, to go to the opening ceremony, and to speak to many gifted, wonderful sports people – I absolutely loved it. But then I lost in the first round [to Lu Yen-hsun of Taiwan].

When I weighed myself the night after my loss, I discovered I'd lost five kilos since leaving Cincinnati a week before. I was completely dehydrated. I had not been professional in my approach because I was so excited at being part of the Olympics. I knew that when London came around my attitude had to be different. I was never going to make the Beijing mistake again. I had forgotten I was there to win tennis matches for the country, because I was enjoying the experience so much.

I didn't think that going to the opening ceremony

in Beijing would affect me. It was only in hindsight that I realised I had used up tremendous amounts of energy, speaking to loads of people and enjoying the whole occasion. For some participants that is what the Olympics should be about, but I know how disappointed I was to lose so early because I had a chance to do well for the country and I blew it.

I would have loved to have gone to the London 2012 opening ceremony – it turned out to be the most spectacular event – but it was the wrong thing to do from a professional perspective. I didn't want to make the same mistake twice.

However, I was among the fortunate people nominated to carry the flame on its journey across the nation. That was a tremendous privilege. OK, I was only able to carry it inside the confines of the All England Club, but there were members and players in attendance – I remember Novak Djokovic and Tomáš Berdych cutting short their practice sessions to come and watch me receive the flame.

I love representing Britain and the Olympics gave me a chance to show how much. I wanted to play in the singles, doubles, mixed doubles – I wanted to do everything and feel all of the sensations of being a part of Team GB.

My first match against Stanislas Wawrinka of Switzerland was a really tough one. I had been practising with him so often beforehand . . . and killing him actually! In those ten days, I think I had won every practice set and I had just felt great generally.

When I'm playing abroad – at the US Open, say – I don't really feel so much that I am representing my country. At Wimbledon I certainly do and all the associated pressure that goes with it. But there was so much going on during the Games, the tennis aspect was only one small part of it, and I got the benefit of that – the motivation was just as great, I was pumped to do well – but the pressure seemed less intense somehow.

I watched as many of the other sports as I could when I wasn't playing, and I wanted to try to be a part of that success. When I lose at the Wimbledon Championships, there isn't usually anyone else left for British fans to support; if I'd have lost at the Olympics, there was still Bradley Wiggins, Mo Farah, Jessica Ennis and Chris Hoy. If I had lost, I doubt whether people would have spent much time talking about it, because there were so many other exciting things going on elsewhere to concentrate on.

The night before playing in the final, I watched

Ennis, Farah and Greg Rutherford all win gold in the Olympic Stadium. The atmosphere was outrageous, it was crackling. The country was alive with optimism, there was momentum and everyone was so positive, from the spectators to the media.

In advance of the Games, the stories had all been about the prospect of terrible traffic problems, potential security problems and ticketing issues. People thought the opening ceremony would not be as good as in Beijing, but it proved to be an incredible spectacle.

Then a few days in, it was all: 'We haven't won a gold yet'. Everything was negative again. But once the first gold arrived, then another, then a couple more, it all changed. There was nothing to complain about anymore and the whole nation was carried along on a wave of excitement. The athletes performed better than anyone was expecting – career-best performances, golds, silvers, glorious achievements – and I put a lot of that down to the positive momentum all around. As an individual sportsman, I'd certainly never experienced anything like it.

I managed to make good progress through my first four rounds, only losing one set to Marcos Baghdatis, who challenged me really hard again. Then, after I defeated Nicolás Almagro of Spain on No.1 Court, with the Duke and Duchess of Cambridge amongst the spectators, I was into the semi-finals to play Novak again. I spoke to Ivan the evening before and his message was the same as usual: to impose my game on the match, play the game on my terms and not to lose running around with my arse against the back fence.

I managed to execute the game plan, turning in one of my most complete performances of the year. In windy conditions I thought I struck the ball really well. In the first set there were some tremendous rallies, but the second set, by comparison, wasn't quite as good. Novak had a lot of break points, but I served really well and hung tough in those moments and just managed to get the break myself in the end.

The atmosphere was unbelievable, different to anything I'd experienced before. I'd always said that the night matches at the US Open had the best atmosphere, but they weren't even close to what it was like against Novak.

I celebrated victory in the normal way until I sat down in the chair. Suddenly, I leapt up again, as if electricity was surging through my body. I'd realised I had guaranteed myself an Olympic medal.

The final would be a rematch against Roger for Olympic gold. It was being billed as a revenge mission, but going into matches trying to get revenge for something that's happened in the past actually doesn't help at all. I always try to focus on the task in hand and not dwell on what I should or might have done before. There is nothing you can do to bring it back.

One thing that I appreciated might make a difference was that Roger had not played for an Olympic gold in the singles before. Almost every other time I had played him, he had experienced the situations way, way more times than me. It's so rare for him to be in a position where he's trying to do something new because he's experienced and achieved so much in tennis. I hoped that would level the playing field psychologically.

Of course, I would need to play fantastic tennis to win and I wanted it to be a great match because I think the way the matches went on semi-finals day the tournament deserved a great final and I hoped we could provide that.

Roger had beaten Juan Martín del Potro 3-6, 7-6, 19-17 in the other semi-final. At four hours and 26 minutes, it was the longest match in Olympic history and one of the finest matches ever seen on

Centre Court. It was a truly amazing spectacle – and some of the rallies had to be seen to be believed. Juan Martín took his defeat like the big man he is, and Roger got very emotional after his win. Perhaps, like me, that was partly due to the enormous relief that he was going to win an Olympic medal. Coming into the semi-finals, with the quality of players in that last four, there was definitely no guarantee of that. Though I really wanted to win gold, I wanted to at least come away with a medal. If I had lost the semi-final, I would have been playing Juan Martín for the bronze and that would have been very tough, as Novak discovered, losing and walking away with nothing to show for his efforts. After what had happened to me at Wimbledon a month before, that would have been another huge let down.

Laura Robson and I were progressing well in the mixed doubles, too. The day before my singles final we had to play twice, defeating two Australian Grand Slam champions, Lleyton Hewitt and Sam Stosur, in the quarter-final and Christopher Kas and Sabine Lisicki of Germany in the semis. It was good to spend the day occupied with something other than thinking about how the singles might go, even better to finish it with the guarantee of another medal. In the final, we would play Max Mirnyi and Victoria Azarenka from Belarus. Had the singles been best-of-five sets throughout, I would not have been able to play all three events, but with best-of-three format and the doubles scoring, it was all quick and I wanted to try to win as many medals as I could. If I won the mixed doubles at the US Open, no one would be that fussed. To me this was a really big deal, and the same went for Laura.

● ● ●

The atmosphere on finals day was nerve-tingling once again. So many were decked out in Union Jack colours, every spectator seemed to have a flag. I would imagine for Roger, the fact that the fans were so obviously in my corner must have been a shock for him. He's been on that court so many times and the British have great affection for him. The Wimbledon final was fairly split, but in the Olympics the support for me was amazing. When the crowd is right behind you, it does make a huge difference – it makes you perform better, the opponent can feel intimidated, and when things are going well it is easier to carry that momentum through a match. Against Roger, this time, I didn't let up at all.

The middle part of the match was, without doubt, the best I'd played in my career to that point. I'm not saying Roger played his best match, but the support of the crowd and the momentum from everyone else in every other sport doing so well seemed to carry me along. I just felt right the whole match.

I finished it with three big serves in a row. I think he only got a racket on a couple of them. I was serving for the biggest title of my career and I served as well as I had ever done.

In the moments after a special match like this there are certain people you want to be with. Not everyone got to see what I was really like after Wimbledon, even though Kim and my mum and dad would have known how I was feeling. They had seen me lose so many of those matches before. That made me doubt myself – and maybe they doubted me as well – so it was great to be able to spend two or three seconds with them straight after I'd won. They knew all the work that went into the victory and how many tough losses there had been along the way. Out of all of the things that happened to me in 2012, winning the gold medal was the proudest moment.

There had been four weeks to the day between one of the hardest moments of my life and one of the most fulfilling. Roger was involved in both of them and he made them special because he's arguably the greatest of all time.

I was nervous before the final of the Olympics but I don't remember feeling the same fear as before at Wimbledon. Maybe when I was playing on Centre Court before I felt I had to behave myself, because everyone was watching me and maybe I felt a bit self-conscious. People weren't necessarily waiting for me to slip up but if I did, somebody would have something to say about it and everyone would have an opinion on what I had or hadn't done. But after Wimbledon, people accepted my flaws – and I have loads of them. People seemed to see me for what I am and how I express myself, not judge me on what I should or shouldn't do.

I remember shaking my head when I was up there on the podium, ready to receive the medal. All of the guys in my team were there and the podiums were set up so that I was facing them. Seeing them all smiling, and everyone looking so proud, made me feel wonderful. Yes, I was proud of myself, but when I saw everyone else smiling and everyone singing the national anthem, I got a real sense of togetherness. Maybe we don't show enough of that in our country, and maybe the result is that sometimes we don't get a sense that everyone can pull together for the same cause. When I saw Sir Chris Hoy holding the flag at the opening ceremony and he was completely blubbing the whole way around, I realised that you don't get that in other competitions and that the London Olympics was really special.

I had a ticket for the 100 metres final that night, but ended up missing it because of the mixed doubles final. Laura and I tried our hardest and even played another championship tie-break – our third in a row – but this time Max Mirnyi and Victoria Azarenka were just too good for us and we ended up taking a silver.

I had to content myself with watching Usain Bolt power to victory on TV and then we headed over to the Olympic Village to do all the media commitments By the time we were done it was extremely late and we didn't get home until 3.30am.

Even after a day like that, I still had to be up at 6.30 to do more press. Mind you, it's a lot easier to get up and face the world the morning after winning.

I wanted to show off my gold medal. I went to the National Tennis Centre the next day and all the people in there wanted to do was to touch the medal.

It wasn't as if I was particularly protective of it, because it felt like I'd won it for everyone. I was proud of myself and, without wishing to sound stupid, I was proud of the country as well. We'd done well.

I would have loved to stay in Britain to enjoy the atmosphere for longer. As I had been through so many disappointments in my career, I wanted to enjoy the moment. But that's not how tennis works, and the same day I had to leave for Montreal.

Canada is a wonderful country, but I was frustrated when I got there this time because their TV channels were focusing on their athletes at the Olympics. I couldn't get to see any more of Team GB and that was all I wanted to do that week, along with the rest of the country. The demands of my sport also meant that I missed all the open-top bus rides, the celebrations. I didn't even get to the closing ceremony. The closest I came was calling Chris Hoy to talk about how much I had loved being a part of it. He said how amazing it was and that it would never get any better. Who knew if it ever would?

The racket has gone, that hat is about
to follow. It's two seconds since I became
Wimbledon champion and my reaction
is completely spontaneous.

(Top) I couldn't see into the BBC commentary box so the first faces I recognised were those of the British tennis writers.

(Bottom) Trying to work out exactly what I had done. These are very public moments but you want a sense of privacy too. I was just so incredibly happy.

Novak Djokovic is a true champion.
He came around to my side of the
court to greet me, but I honestly don't
remember what either he or I said.

(Top) One of the great joys of the day, as I got to share my success with a lot of people I didn't know and who didn't know me. I was high-fiving total strangers.

(Bottom) Arthur Ashe Stadium: the biggest, nosiest, most raucous tennis court in the world. It's not everyone's cup of tea but I love the sessions here, especially at night.

The immediate aftermath of the 2008 US Open final when I lost in straight sets to Roger Federer. I pushed him as hard as I could but he had all the answers that day.

So many people have helped me along the way. Mark Petchey was like an older brother; he gave up a lot for me and I'll always be grateful.

For someone so young, Dani Vallverdu is a great organiser. He knows the game inside out. He'll do anything he can for me and he's a true friend.

I love the look on everyone's faces here during the 2012 US Open final. I think Matt Gentry, the managing director of my new company 77 (middle top), is trying to out-Fergie Sir Alex Ferguson.

(Left) A peck for the US Open Junior Boys' trophy. I beat Sergiy Stakhovsky of Ukraine in the final. (Right) With the Sony Ericsson Open trophy

Some more trophies.
Clockwise, from top left:
Thailand Open, Brisbane
International, Western and
Southern Open and the
Qatar ExxonMobil.

CHAPTER 4

Two days after the Olympic final, though, I was playing in Canada. My body hurt, I was stiff and felt sore, so I didn't have enough time to enjoy it. In the end, I won a match in Toronto before I pulled out with bad twinges in my back and then lost to Jérémy Chardy in Cincinnati. That's two Masters tournaments back to back and I just wasn't in an especially good place. The guys in the team were asking what was wrong and whether we should go down to Miami to train and spend a few days there. I must have seemed so down on the court, but I ended up telling them: 'No, I'm fine, trust me – when the US Open comes, there won't be any performances like that.' I wanted to show them that I just needed to get to New York and then I'd be OK.

After I arrived in New York I didn't see any of the guys for a couple of days. That gave me a chance to lose myself in the city for 48 hours. I went to Whole Foods for my dinner, which was something that has become a bit of a habit for me in the United States, and walked around Central Park. My downtime gave me a chance to watch some of the Premier League football on TV. Fantasy Football was starting up again for the new season, so I had a go at that and just enjoyed being on my own for the first time in ages.

It's rare that I don't see anyone for a couple of days. I'm always surrounded by people – from my team, members of the press, tournament staff and family members. I rarely get to do any of the tourist things, or just go for a stroll, so I enjoyed having a bit of 'me' time.

By Tuesday, though, we were all back together again and it was time to start the real preparation.

The US Open has always been a tournament I've felt a special affinity for. It started from when I was a junior. I can remember staying up into the small hours when I was about 14 to watch the quarter-final between Andre Agassi and Pete Sampras. It was Sampras who won 6-7, 7-6, 7-6, 7-6 and it ended up being an amazing game. The energy generated by these two players under the lights at Arthur Ashe Stadium felt like magic and it was something I wanted to experience for myself. Three years later, I was the junior champion there, defeating Sergiy Stakhovsky from the Ukraine. He went on to beat Roger Federer in the second round of Wimbledon the year I won it, so you could say that we ended up being quite closely connected.

I was taken to the top of the stadium to look down on the court, and that has to be one of the greatest sights in tennis.

The difference at the US Open was that juniors and senior players were allowed to mix, so we could hang out and be around the star players. The juniors were treated really well and we stayed at a lovely hotel. I was introduced to Guillermo Coria of Argentina, who was my favourite player at the time, and even managed to watch Tim Henman and Roger Federer playing on the putting machine before their semi-final. Then I went out to watch the match in the crowd and it was so different to anything else I had ever experienced before. As a kid at the French Open I felt slightly out of the way, maybe a bit disconnected, and at Wimbledon the juniors stayed at the Roehampton Institute. The result is that you don't feel as if it is such a massive deal to be there. That isn't the way of it at the US Open. I felt I was almost there as a senior player, almost as though I'd made it. And that gave me great motivation to take the next steps.

The two main stadiums there are called Arthur Ashe and Louis Armstrong. One I love, the other I have never felt comfortable on. I just don't like Armstrong and never have. Each time I've played on it I've struggled, and the 2012 championship was a case in point. I started strongly enough, beating Alex Bogomolov and Ivan Dodig in the first two rounds on Ashe and then had to play Feliciano López of Spain over on Armstrong. And the jinx almost held because I couldn't really settle properly. It can get breezy on the big courts; on Ashe it generally blows from the President's Box end and you get used to that, but on Armstrong, where there's no sense of being enclosed, the wind swirls and moves in different directions. You are more exposed to the sun playing day matches on Armstrong, too, and it can be so bright that tracking the ball gets really hard.

The grandstand in the Arthur Ashe Stadium gives

more shelter from the wind and it's built so that the sun moves across early in the day, providing plenty of shadow and shade. On Armstrong the sun is on the players for the whole day and it's really intense. That made it difficult for me to settle, but the fact is that López is not much fun to play. He had Àlex Corretja, a former coach of mine, in his box. I spoke to Àlex afterwards and he said that 'Feli' played a really tough match, served really well and made it difficult for me. As a result, I struggled physically, but somehow it was one of those matches that I found a way to win. I didn't feel right at all, but somehow I got through. I used to be able to do that a lot of times in all the regular tournaments I played on tour and managed to get a really high degree of consistency throughout the year. However, in the Slams that wasn't necessarily the case. Now I've learned how to cope in situations when the pressure is on. I think about how my opponent might be feeling. I understand it all much better than I did before.

In the fourth round, I played well against a new big gun on the tour, Milos Raonic of Canada. We were playing on Ashe at night, which I really like. The conditions seem kinder in the evening and that was one of those really good nights. I read his serve well from early on and seemed to be able to anticipate everything he was going to do. I was moving really well, which you have to when you play guys who have big, accurate serves. Often when they serve, you get the return back a little short and then you're on the defensive against them. In those games you have to come up with good passing shots, which can take a lot out of you. That night I was quick and in command.

For the quarter-final against Marin Čilić of Croatia, the game was back on Armstrong and the pressure was really on. Čilić made sure that I felt it from the start, taking the first set and going on to take a 5-1 lead in the second.

When I got the first break back in that second set, we both sensed how important the next couple of games would be. And I started to feel that he was getting nervous. After that, I played on pure instinct. I got to balls I hadn't been reaching before, chased everything down and got back into the match the hard way.

Perhaps if he hadn't got nervous I wouldn't have won, but there were nerves for me too. If you sense the opponent is tightening up and think, 'I can get back in here, this is my chance', the pressure increases on you. The guys who are behind aren't the ones who tend to rush. They have all the time in the world, which is why it was surprising to see him hurry and make mistakes. It wasn't as if I was blasting winners all over the court, so much as making as many balls as I could. Little by little, I started to reclaim the middle of the court, and he started to miss. That was it.

The semi-final against Tomáš Berdych of the Czech Republic on Ashe was a freak show. There were high winds, which meant that, for me, it wasn't proper tennis – in which it's all about who hits the ball best that day. It was about who could manoeuvre the ball around and come up with the right shots and the smartest shots. I feel like I have a bit more variety in my game than Tomáš, so the conditions helped me and hindered him more than me. It was almost comical because of the wind conditions and I was laughing a little inside at how ridiculous the points were. All the same, it was the semi-final of the US Open, and it was a great opportunity.

I aced Berdych when the ball bounced twice before it reached him. That has never happened the whole time I've been on the tour, but there was stuff taking place out there that had never happened in my entire life. If you had wanted to, you could easily have spun the ball from your opponent's court back onto your own side because the breeze was so strong. Once in Las Vegas I had to warm up in similar conditions, but this was an actual match.

Playing a proper point became impossible and, in all the chaos, I managed to lose the first set. After that, I felt like I was cruising. I took the second and third sets easily and I had two break points in the third. Then Berdych started to serve and volley with much greater consistency, coming into the net more. After that, things changed quickly. I was 5-7, 6-2, 6-1 up and he had enough break points to put me 5-1 down in the fourth. That was the point where I started the fight back and ended up taking it to a tie-break.

I went 5-2 down in that and realised that I'd gone from a commanding position to win the match to one where it looked likely to go into a fifth set. I'd had all the momentum with me, and then I was on the verge of blowing it through my bad play and his consistency. The conditions were ridiculous, but that's no excuse because it was the same for both of us. It was so, so difficult, but I fought back and won. I was just pleased to get it over and done with.

My post-match press conference took a surreal

turn. I knew that both Sir Sean Connery and Sir Alex Ferguson had been at the match, but I wasn't expecting to suddenly be confronted by both of them. I had spoken to Sean Connery on the phone before the game, but I'd never even met Alex Ferguson. That made it a weird situation and, to be honest, I didn't know what to say to either of them. Both are quite intimidating presences in their own way. I've seen Sir Alex on TV so many times – in the dugout, doing post-match interviews – and it seems like he's really intense. You get the feeling that if you say the wrong thing when he's doing his job, he's going to bite your head off.

But he came into the press conference with a massive smile on his face. He was really relaxed – I think he might have had a couple of drinks – so it was cool. I didn't say much because I was too much in awe. What he's accomplished at Manchester United will probably never happen again in football: the success he has had, the trophies he's won and the reputation he's earned commands massive respect. Throughout my whole career I've had an appreciation of what he's done and, because he's been such an ever-present for United, it's like he's been in the front room. Getting to meet him and spend a bit of time with him was an honour and made me realise that not only is he an amazing person, he's also very interesting to talk to.

What I didn't realise then was that my mum had arranged for him to be in my box at the final. It was great that he was there and came along to provide his support and I'm sure that if I thought about it normally, it would give me a huge lift. But when I was on court at that stage of my career, I had to make sure that I wasn't unnerved by it. I had to work hard to get myself into that position and I wasn't going to let anything distract me.

Nonetheless, before the match was the worst I've ever felt by far. After I finished practising, I ate in the locker room. The guys went up to get some food and I found myself alone for 20 minutes, feeling sick with nerves and worry. A lot of people said that winning the Olympics would mean the pressure was off, but they had no idea. I was sitting there and feeling really ill. I got up and moved around and tried to think about other stuff, which is why it's useful to have people around me. They might be talking about something else and though I'm still going to be thinking about the match, at least there's a distraction. The more I started thinking about how big the match was for me, the more nervous I became.

Novak doesn't usually stay in the locker room and seems to go elsewhere, although I don't know where. There was no one else there apart from a couple of the attendants, and the physiotherapy room was closed because there was nobody left to treat. There were no doubles players in there, no mixed teams and the only sound was coming from the TV. The guy on there was saying that no one had ever lost their first five Grand Slam finals. I knew that, of course, but to hear it in those circumstances just added to my nerves.

I had spoken to Ivan about nerves before and he said that he found it especially hard before the US Open final, because you have the whole day to kill beforehand. He would go in, warm up, leave, play a round of golf, come back, warm up a little again and then play. He did say that he felt nervous before each of his finals, which I suppose is re-asssuring. Some people say that pressure is a privilege and you ought to enjoy it, but when you haven't won one of those events it doesn't necessarily feel that way. Ultimately, you have to believe that it'll be fine win or lose, but because of the way that

Wimbledon finished, a loss in this final could have been very tough.

When Novak and I finally walked out onto court, the wind was blowing strongly into our faces. The Berdych match had been ridiculous because the wind was going every which way, but at least this time it was coming consistently from one direction. It's normally good to play with the wind, but that day it was so strong. The balls are pretty light and from the President's Box side it was hard to keep the ball in court.

It felt like no time until we were involved in a first-set tie-break. Maybe it was one of those classics from the sidelines, but to actually play in it was a lot more trying, especially because both of us found that it was so much harder to execute the shots we wanted to. Novak had the odd chance, but it would have been tough to lose after having so many set points. I needed to win to have a realistic shot at winning the match. In the end, I took the tie-break 12-10. We'd already been playing for more than an hour.

At two sets to love up, I was elated but I couldn't let myself relax. By the beginning of the third set, the wind had settled completely. Novak had been struggling before, but when the wind calmed, I had the sense that it calmed him too. By that stage, I was just one set away from victory and feeling that, with the conditions the way they were, they'd been a big help. He had been getting frustrated, so when the wind died and the air stilled, he started to hit out on his shots with more confidence. He was more comfortable and moving better and that made me nervous.

Those nerves and Novak's confidence changed the way I had to play the match. He won two sets, and I recall shouting out that my legs felt like jelly because they wouldn't move where I wanted them to. Once I got that out of my system, I was OK again.

At the end of the fourth set, I decided to take a toilet break. There's a toilet right there at the side of the court and I knew that by taking a break, all the people would be thinking: 'He's blown this one.'

When I was walking off, I was pretty down. We had been playing for four hours but what matters most is how much you've run, because you're not moving for the entirety of the time. The temperature had dropped and even though there were long points, I was making him do most of the running. At the end of the fourth, I think he was struggling physically more than I was.

In the bathroom, I looked at myself in the mirror

and said: 'I'm not going to lose this' (well, something along those lines – I can't remember the exact words). For me, it was about going back out to give 100 per cent and leave nothing behind. No regrets.

I came back out and looked over at Ivan in the box. That fired me up because I wanted to win so badly, maybe more than him, if only because I'd never won before. I wasn't going to let myself lose that match from that position, the way Wimbledon had gone.

I secured a break in the first game, when Novak missed a forehand after a net cord at 30–40. Then I made it a double break to put myself 3–0 up. He then got a break back. Even I haven't watched much of the match on DVD, but I do remember that I had a great service game to love to lead 4–2 and then backed that up with a break to lead 5–2.

I had built it up so much in my head that it would be a big thing to serve for a Grand Slam, but when it came to it I didn't feel that nervous. I had two breaks and when I looked up I could see the spectators were going nuts. I was feeding off all that energy. I was actually speaking to people in the crowd – I don't know if it made much sense, it was probably just something to get me fired up. Even though I'd never been in that position before, even though I'd spent quite a bit of time wondering how it might feel, I felt oddly calm.

The score got to 40-love and I was about to win. I've been in that position loads of times and, 99 times out of 100, I hold serve. With the wind in my favour, I went to the wrong side to serve because I was concentrating so hard and I didn't realise quite where I was. On the first Championship point, he threw up a lob, I got the rim of the racket to it and he hit a winner. On the next point, he smacked his return and I knew 100 per cent that it was out, but thought he'd challenge. I heard the call, saw the ball and my reaction was pure disbelief.

It took a while to understand what it meant to win the US Open. Maybe, after everything, it wasn't as big as I had built it up to be, but I was so relieved to have finally done it, that I felt a mix of pure elation and disbelief. The one thing I would have liked to have done afterwards, in front of the TV cameras, was to thank everyone who has supported and worked with me, but time was too short. It was in the locker room that our celebrations began. There were hugs and kisses and I just remember there being lots of banter. Ivan was smiling more than I'd ever seen him smile and he told me how proud he was of what I had done. He also said that I had shown great fighting spirit and played an excellent match, which, coming from him, was exactly what I wanted to hear. He didn't want to join the rest of the team for dinner that night, but seemed to go home very happy.

We had a great night. I slept for about an hour, having read as many stories about the match as I could online before I finally drifted off, only to be woken by an early alarm call ready for a round of media appearances.

That night, I treated myself to an upgrade on the flight home. Everyone else was asleep and I just couldn't make myself drop off. I had a glass of champagne, which I never do, and that became four. I actually mistook the soap in the bathroom for toothpaste because I was a bit giddy. If there were any bumps on the flight home, I certainly didn't feel them.

5

CHAPTER 5

There is a relentlessness that goes with being me. I have a sense that what I do is never good enough. Perhaps that's what keeps me playing. But going into Wimbledon this year, it felt different. Better than a year ago. A year ago it felt better than three or four years ago. And so I've coped better with the growing-up process during that time. So much of it has happened in the public eye with the media, the pressure and the scrutiny. That's part of the job as a professional tennis player, but it's also part of what goes with being the central figure in British tennis these past few years.

I've known all along that being in the media

comes with that territory, but I've always tried to play that side of things down in an attempt to keep it under control. But when I'm building up to the big tournaments, that's when I really feel it. I can sense the demands, the pressures and peoples' expectations of me. Maybe they even *expect* me to win, and that's hard.

I try to block everything out and get rid of all that from my mind. For that whole time, I'm not listening to the media and not reading the newspapers. But every week before the Wimbledon Championships begin, as I mentioned earlier, I start to get terrible mouth ulcers and I don't get them at any other time. The mouth ulcers can be nasty and they reflect how much I'm feeling the stress. Thankfully they usually go quite soon.

What has made that pressure worse is that after the early rounds I'm usually the only British man left in the singles. I have heard it called an impossible burden, but I've learned to live with it. If I wasn't bothered or worried, I could go out and play in complete freedom but it is not that easy. I have seen how it has affected others, especially how Tim Henman had to deal with it, and I think it really knocked him back. That's what I want to avoid, but then it isn't always that straightforward.

I care about the sport, but then I've spent so much time playing and investing in it. And I also care about tennis in this country and how it's viewed, which means that I put additional pressure on myself. Maybe I put that extra weight on myself because I don't want the sport to be addressed in a poor light. For the past few years, I don't think tennis has been viewed particularly positively in this country for a range of different reasons, and it feels like me being beaten would make matters worse.

One thing that I'd say about myself is that as high as all the expectations are, I've always played close to my best tennis around Wimbledon. The scrutiny might be extremely intense, but when I've stepped out onto the court I've harnessed that pressure and performed well. Maybe it is, in a really strange way, a factor that I have to take as a positive.

The pressure really started when I first came through. There were Tim and Greg and they took most of the attention, but then that changed. They retired and suddenly the focus was all on me. It was really, really hard going through that process and learning how to deal with it. Growing up in the spotlight isn't something I'd wish on anyone because it doesn't allow you to make any mistakes without being publicly criticised in loads of different ways. To be honest, you probably see it a bit less in sport, but if you're a young musician, a pop star or an actor, then that's going to be so hard. When some of them become successful they surround themselves with the wrong people and end up in a mess. That's something I've consciously tried to avoid. You need the people around you to safe-guard you and basically create a protective bubble. Nobody else who might want to influence you negatively or make you do stupid things should be allowed to come into that bubble.

On the tour, you see a lot of players go in front of TV and put on cheesy grins and smile and act like the nicest people in the world. Then when the cameras are off, they're completely different. Maybe it's easy to do that: people telling you that you need to smile more when the media are around and be nice to them. But to be honest, I'm not a natural. I smile enough away from the cameras when there's something that I want to smile about and I don't have to do it because people want me to. Being like that has made my life a lot simpler.

The first few times I played Wimbledon, I had people following me around everywhere I went. If you happen not to be where the news and sports cameras are, then it's the paparazzi who are following you. And if you step out of the car and do something outrageous, then they're going to keep following you. But if you lead a normal life, you walk the dogs and stay at home, then they're going to get bored and stop. In my case, I'm not looking to get in the papers or seek out fame.

● ● ●

When people ask me if I think I've ever had an effect on other people, for better or for worse, it's really hard to know how to answer that and to place myself in that kind of position. I have read some things about how my experiences may have had an influence on other people, but it'd be really arrogant to say that I've helped to shape their lives.

When I was in Florida in December 2012, preparing hard for the Australian Open, I heard about the tragedy at the Sandy Hook Elementary School in Newtown, Connecticut. Like anyone else, watching the scenes unfold on television and the whole episode was pretty upsetting, especially if you took the time to think yourself into the position of the children or their parents. I posted a message of support on

Facebook and tried to get my head around what would make the shooter act in such a shocking way and end up ruining so many lives, forever.

I read an account of how a pastor had helped provide support for one British family, the Hockleys, who had lost their six-year-old son Dylan. Apparently he had used the story of what happened in my home town of Dunblane in 1996, when I was nine years old, as an element of what he hoped would be the healing process. He said he told the family the story of a little boy from another small town who had cowered under a desk as this guy went on the rampage around the school. He said that boy and his town had risen from the ashes and rebuilt for the future. He said that town was Dunblane and that boy was me.

That was very nice, very touching and very humbling. I can't imagine what the families are going through because every situation is different and everyone experiences the emotions involved differently. I think you process that stuff in your own way, depending on who you are: there's no right or wrong way to deal with it.

When I'm asked about what happened a long time ago, back in my own school, I don't really want to get involved in talking about it. It's part of my history which I can't get away from, and a lot of people want to talk to me and ask about it, but they have to recognise that you can't just turn those emotions off and on for every interviewer who wants to talk to you. It's just too hard.

If you saw the BBC documentary I did with Sue Barker earlier this year, you'll have recognised the emotions and that's all I want to say about it. The future is what matters most and seeing the town now, seeing how Dunblane has risen: that fills me with massive pride.

● ● ●

I had a great childhood, surrounded by a devoted family and always with things to do. But there are kids who are brought up in a rough neighbourhood by parents who just don't have the right skills, and we have to listen to those kids. We need to try to help them and not just write them off, because otherwise we'd be turning our backs on loads of potential.

The people who have followed me for a long time, well, I hope they understand and don't judge me too harshly for my failings. Everyone has flaws. I don't claim to be perfect, nobody is. You're always going to fall short of the ideal. As you grow up in the goldfish bowl, you start to understand things a bit more clearly. You see how, over time, certain things that really aggravated you before don't mean as much. When I was younger I didn't necessarily understand how the press worked and I used to worry about what they said. Now, if I play rubbish and they write that I played rubbish, that's fine. I play tennis and they write about it.

A lot of my fans follow me on social media. The ones who really know me are the ones who take a real interest in my career. They take the time to know what I'm really like, what my upbringing has been and what I've gone through. They know my story and will understand why I am the way I am. Maybe that's down to what happened in Dunblane when I was too young to understand much. Maybe it's down to my parents, or my decision to move away to Spain and get some independence. The true fans understand all those complexities and see me for what I am rather than trying to find the perfect human being.

It seems like that's what some people want to see these days. Whether it's the woman with the perfect figure, or a man with fantastic features, so many of them seem to want to be in the limelight and be famous for being famous. To me, that's weird. Life goes a lot deeper than that. What counts are your values as a person rather than how you appear in front of the cameras.

That reality is what made going back to Dunblane after my success in the Olympics and my victory at the US Open so special. I had no idea what it was going to be like, and joked to a friend the night before that it'd be funny if there were only two people in front of the butcher's.

On the morning of the occasion, I was really nervous. When I'm on the court I'm used to being the centre of attention, but it's not like the people who are watching you can come up and talk to you while you're playing. Everyone knows what their roles are. When I'm not playing tennis, that person who's the centre of attention is not me at all. If I sit down at the dinner table I'm not the one making all the noise and the conversation doesn't centre around me. That made me wonder how it might be in Dunblane.

In the end, what happened was really emotional and gave me a massive lift. I appreciate now and certainly felt then that it wasn't about me, but a celebration of everyone in the town. I got to see people that I wouldn't have thought about for a long time and saw all the teachers from my school. Even the newsagent I used to pinch penny sweets from gave me a free choice of what I wanted, which was really funny. When I sat down with the kids next to the post box they had painted gold in honour of my Olympic medal, everyone could see the delight as they wore the medals. That's when I knew it was a day for a lot of people to relish. It just happened to be me in the middle, but the day was for them, not for me. It was a day to celebrate much more than winning a few tennis matches.

I saw Fuzzy, who is the hairdresser in town, and he told me I must have had a decent cut recently because my hair was all over the place in New York. I went up to the tennis club which used to be empty all the time and there were hundreds of kids up there. And the finishing touch was that it was raining. That was fitting because it was always the way I remembered it there. It did show that all you need are courts and enthusiastic grown-ups to have kids enjoying tennis, no matter what the elements. It might not have been a beautiful day for the weather, but it was in every other respect.

I've become a property owner in the area now. A guy called Neil Grainger looks after my finances.

His first client was Sue Barker and he did an awful lot for Tim Henman as well, so he's often trying to get me to do various things with my money. For me, property is interesting because at least I know what I'm buying, but I don't understand the stock market at all. Some people have made a fortune but others have got completely burned, which is a bit scary for me.

But, when the opportunity came up to buy a hotel in the area, I thought it would be a really nice thing to do. My brother Jamie was married there, my grandparents had a big anniversary celebration there. But the place had got completely run down which was a real shame because it was a really nice hotel.

I spoke to Neil about it and initially he was a bit reluctant. Then he went to see it and spoke to a few people in the area and came back sounding much more positive. It is a cool thing for my family to be involved in and it would have been such a shame had it been sold to people from outside the area who might have used it as a house for two or three months of the year and then left it empty. Now, there will be more jobs created in the area, and any of my friends or family can go there to stay or be entertained.

My investment in the property was pretty big

and the hotel aspect of it will, hopefully, start to make a decent profit over a period of time. That won't happen for the first few years, but I don't mind because it'll be something rewarding for me when I'm done playing. It'll also be somewhere to go and stay when I'm back home. It's only five minutes from where I grew up and a really beautiful place.

● ● ●

I've mentioned Dunblane, and how something positive came out of an experience that was pretty horrific. Everyone involved, me included, will have learned a lot from the experience and come out stronger. It's similar to what happened to my friend Ross Hutchins in December 2012.

He messaged me just before Christmas and in retrospect, I can see why a phone call would not have been very pleasant. I had just landed in London from training in Miami and I was going back to Scotland that evening for a few days over the holiday. Ross really wanted to meet up, but I texted back: 'I'm tired, jet-lagged, I have to go to Scotland tonight.' He sent a message back saying: 'OK, no worries, we'll talk again soon – have a great Christmas'.

I did have a great time at home. It was very relaxing, but before I knew it I was on my way out to Abu Dhabi on Christmas evening. When I arrived there, Ross messaged me again, saying could we talk and that he had discovered he had a type of cancer called Hodgkin's lymphoma. I looked at the message a few times and it took a while to sink in. I was obviously very upset for him and my first thought was that I knew I'd be heading down to Australia for a month straight after Abu Dhabi. I knew a little about cancer and how quickly it could spread in the very worst cases, so I realised that I should have made time to see him when he messaged me in the first place.

When I got to Brisbane I was messaging him every single day and looking into the exact nature of this particular form of cancer, and was trying to find other cases of athletes who had had it and recovered. Maybe it would help him if he could look at who had come out on the other side and know that he'd make it.

I beat Grigor Dimitrov of Bulgaria in a really good final and at the end of my speech on court, my voice shaking with emotion, I dedicated my victory to one of my best friends 'who is back home watching – and you're going to get through'. I had signed something on the camera lens which provoked a lot of interest because people were trying to decipher my handwriting. It wasn't at its best and I don't even recall what I wrote, but it would have been for Ross.

As soon as I said what I did, everyone was trying to find out who and what I was referring to. That prompted Ross to say that he was the friend and announce what had happened. I heard that he gave a conference call to the British writers who had already arrived in Australia for the Open and spoke with such frankness, honesty and positivity about what was happening to him. That's typical of him. He's such a strong, open character.

The way it affected me was that I stopped worrying about myself as much. Ross would message me over the following days and weeks and those messages, amazingly, largely consisted of him asking me how *I* was doing. In the past, I might have said to myself: 'I'm really tired, I'm playing crap and it's rubbish,' but when someone is fighting cancer, and nothing that bad has ever affected me before, you think twice and realise life isn't that bad. When I lost in the Australian Open final, I was gutted but I got a message from Ross straight afterwards saying how well I had done and how proud of me he was. I suddenly realised that my predicament was not that bad, it's just a tennis match.

People talk about cancer all the time but until it directly affects you, you don't understand its serious implications. After what happened with Ross and his diagnosis, it was an eye opener not just to me but to many of the other players who know him well. We've probably all realised that we're extremely fortunate and we need to enjoy what we're are doing because, out of the blue, you can get news like that.

In Shanghai that year Ross had been in so much pain that he couldn't sleep. He would be sleeping on the ground but he was still winning matches. Each day, he'd practise with Colin Fleming and I played a few points with him as well. There were times when he couldn't serve because his back was so sore, but he never complained.

When Ross started the chemotherapy, he dealt with everything unbelievably well, but for all that you could see he was sick. That was really tough because it was the first time I had seen him since his diagnosis. I wanted to be so positive and happy but it was difficult to see him like that. He went through the whole of chemo and I know that he's extremely grateful to the doctors and nurses at the Royal Marsden Hospital in Sutton, Surrey. They've been there with him through the entire experience and I could not have been happier to be even a small part of that.

We held the Rally Against Cancer at Queen's after the 2013 Aegeon Championships to raise money for the Royal Marsden. It's about the only way we could all think of to help directly. It ended up being a true coming together of people from sport, business, politics and even comedy with just one thing in mind. The objective was to deliver the funds that can help those like Ross who are trying to deal with this terrible illness.

It was really tough for me to deal with what was happening half the world away. And it was hard for all of the guys around me because they've spent training blocks with Ross as well and he is the nicest guy on the planet. I've never seen him in a bad mood and the way he dealt with the cancer treatment was so amazing. He stayed positive the whole way through it and his family were like that as well. He saw all the right people and followed exactly what he was meant to do.

It was one of the happiest days I can recall when,

soon after Wimbledon, I received a text from Ross saying that he was in remission from cancer. It does not get much better than that. A friend is on the mend, which is another reason for everyone to celebrate.

CHAPTER 6

Retaining my Brisbane International title gave me a lot of confidence going into the 2013 Australian Open. It was my 25th tournament win and it meant a great deal, especially because of what was happening with Ross. That said, there's always a fine line between being confident and being complacent and if you're not careful you can get bitten. But I was in a good place. The Australian Open started well. I didn't get involved in too many long matches and although in the game against Ričardas Berankis he managed to break my serve, I had straight sets victories all the way to the semi-final. That was where I met Roger Federer.

It was a massive step up. I hadn't beaten him in

a Grand Slam – we'd met three times before in Slams and I'd lost on every occasion. I was the third seed, too, so this was where I was supposed to lose.

I took the first set and then Roger took the second on a tie-break. I took the third and then Roger took the fourth, again on a tie-break. By that stage, you know that you're in the heart of a battle and it's going right down to the final set. That's where you have to really make a stand.

There was one incident in the semi-final that received plenty of attention. It was 5-5 in the fourth set and I felt like I was much more in control of the game. I had a shot at winning it there and then and obviously I was keen to do that. We went into the next game and I had a chance to serve out at 6-5. I hit a really good forehand down the line and I think I smiled. Roger didn't like that and shouted something across the court. I didn't see that I had done anything wrong. Stuff like that happens every day in tennis matches. It was very mild in comparison to things that people say on football pitches and in basketball games. So mild, in fact, that I can't even remember what he said.

What I do remember is that Roger really raised his game; and that's the mark of a true champion. He took that set on the tie-break, despite me serving out for the game, and so we went into a fifth set.

You never know what's going to happen next in tennis. The only thing you can do is play the right way, go for your shots when the opportunity is there and hope that it pays off. At any stage, a player of Roger's ability can increase his level and your level can dip, especially in a four-hour match. I just needed to remain as focused as possible, and the beginning of that final set was the part that I was the most pleased with. In the end, I came through 6-2. I did a good job. I think I did all the things that I needed to do and did them well. After the second set and the fourth, which was particularly tough to lose because I felt oddly uncomfortable, I was really pleased with the way that I was able to respond.

After Roger raised his game in the fourth, I just had to tell myself that these things happen. I'd always felt as if I was ahead for the majority of the match, but he hung in really well, and he played some really big points when he was behind. It is what Roger does. It was just great for me to win it, though in retrospect, I had to be on the court for 45 minutes more than I wanted. It doesn't sound like a lot of time but it does take it out of you mentally. You're going to bed an hour or so later and getting a couple of hours less recovery, so that was something to learn from. When I served for the match, I had a chance on the break point and went for a forehand and only just missed it. Maybe I didn't appreciate just then how that game could affect the final, in which case I'd have tried even harder to finish the match off there and then.

I won the first set of the final against Novak Djokovic on a tie-break, but he won the rest. There were some phases of the match when it was really, really close, especially in the second, which went to another tie-break, but I could feel my level dropping. Maybe that was because I'd thrown so much at the semi-final and had slowed down a little, but it was also him playing better as well. If you want to win against those guys, you'd better make sure that you're as fresh as possible, and I just wasn't at all.

There were some obvious reasons for me feeling better about my game after I lost that match. In the build-up to it, I'd been playing some of the best tennis of my life. I made the Wimbledon final, won the US Open and then went close at the Australian. Very close. I knew that nobody had ever won a Slam immediately after winning their first one, but I came very near to achieving that. I had to try to look at all the positives and say to myself that I was moving in the right direction. It was the first time I had beaten Roger in a Slam over five sets and I think I dealt with the ebbs and flows of that match really well. And in the final, I felt much more comfortable on court than I did even during my win at the US Open.

But at that level, it comes down to a few points here and there. My biggest chance? Maybe at the beginning of the second set, but I didn't convert. When Novak got his chance at the end of the third, he took it. And that's the way it is.

His record in the Australian Open is incredible and very few people have managed to dominate it in the way that he has. If you're going to lose, you may as well lose to someone who is a deserved champion.

Thinking back over that tournament, every single game from that end of the court where I was serving for the match against Roger was uphill. I was serving into a slope. The breeze is consistently in one direction, which means you don't have to worry about that element, but from the end of the court where you walk out on Rod Laver Arena you have to do a lot more running. If you watch matches, about 95 per cent of the breaks will come from the guy returning from that end. It is really, really easy to get pushed back from where you want to be. The same is true at the Arthur Ashe Stadium at New York, but the wind changes there. It blows one way one minute and one way the next, which is pretty disconcerting, but my strongest memory of this year's Australian Open was of serving up a slope.

I heard Roger say that my style of play made him doubt himself more than other players, which was really good to hear. He said that no two points were the same and I suppose that is a strength of mine. I'm always looking to keep my opponent moving, thinking and guessing. I think I play tactically smart a lot of the time. That's been something that has always come pretty naturally to me. It was then a question of imposing that over longer periods of matches, to sustain concentration over whole games that go on for hours, even when it's really tough to do.

There's something about playing against Roger. Winning against him at a young age was important and I was 19 when I beat him in straight sets in the second round of Cincinnati in 2006. Once you start going five, six or seven consecutive matches down against someone, it can become a huge mental block.

Beating Roger helped me to believe in myself as a player and, just as importantly, it helped me believe in myself when I played against him in the future. I do have a good record against him. Maybe not so much early in the Slams, but since then we've met 20 times and by the time I went into the 2013 US Open, I still had a winning record against him of 11-9. I'm one of the few to have played him that many times and have a positive record, so that's something special. Roger is one of the best players ever to have stepped onto a tennis court, which makes my achievement all the sweeter.

I enjoy playing against all of the best guys. There are certain matches that are more special, like when I'm playing Roger on grass, Rafa Nadal on a clay court and Novak on a hard court, because their expertise and records on those surfaces are so exceptional. They are pretty incredible athletes. On those specific surfaces against those players, you cannot pick anyone better to play. I have to remember that I'm challenging myself against some of the best players of all time. I've been lucky to have that challenge because it has made me a much better player, that's for sure.

Two matches stand out from all these I've played against Roger. There's the 2012 Wimbledon final and the Olympic final straight after it. The first one had a huge impact on me as a person and as a player. As for the second, it's very rare at this stage of my career to have a totally new experience, but the Olympic final was a new one for both of us.

The only aspect of my tennis career in which I feel I've been unlucky is in all of my Slam finals, I've never played against someone whose experience has been equal to mine: I've never been the most experienced player on the court. These finals have been against Roger and Novak, who have played in many more Slam finals than me, especially Roger. When you look at the records, Roger played Mark Philippoussis in his first Wimbledon final. Novak played Jo-Wilfried Tsonga in Australia in 2008 and Rafa's first final in Paris was against Mariano Puerta. None of those opponents had won a Grand Slam final before, although Mark Philippoussis had previously played Pat Rafter in the US Open final. The important thing is that I was playing guys who knew what it took to win and I still didn't quite know that at the time. So it took me a little longer to gain the experience I needed.

As I mentioned, playing Rafa on clay is always special. The French Open in 2011 was an important tournament for me because I was carrying an ankle injury but still I played very well. It was a close semi-final with a lot of tight games and I didn't feel that I played particularly poorly when the pressure was on. I had a chance at the end of the first set to get back on level terms, but didn't take it. I had several break point opportunities as well, but Rafa played well on most of them. He served strongly and was able to dictate a lot of the points with his forehand. That's the mark of a good player: they play exceptionally well on the big points, and Rafa definitely does that on clay. The match finished up 6-4, 7-5, 6-4 (coincidentally, the same score by which I won the 2013 Wimbledon final against Novak).

Rafa was amazingly aggressive when he needed to be. Playing him at the French Open is probably the toughest test in tennis because his record there is quite amazing. As a competitor, he's definitely among the best. His intensity is the most impressive thing about him. He's had a whole load of success, but he loves the competition, he loves practising and he trains so hard on the court. I've known him since I was very young and though it's hard to be best of friends just now, I'm sure when he finishes playing he's someone about whom I can say we've had a very good relationship over ten years. He is a very respectful competitor. He doesn't look down on anyone or speak badly about any of his opponents. I really admire that.

As with Rafa, the matches I've played with Novak over the last few years have almost always been extremely competitive. They feature long, brutal points in extremely physical matches. To a certain extent, rivalries depend on the surface. His matches with Rafa on clay have been unbelievable, but Rafa and Roger probably have the ultimate match-up because of the contrast in their styles of play. You can see here where the surface plays a part, because Rafa beat him comfortably in the French whereas Roger has the edge when it comes to the indoor tournaments. But when both of them are on their game, whatever surface they happen to be playing on, that is the greatest match to watch.

And when I played Rafa in Australia in 2007, that was definitely a game I look back on as being absolutely key. I lost to him in five sets, which was amazing, because that was the first time I'd played a top player in a Slam. I enjoyed the way that I played, and looking back, it was probably the first time I felt like I could get to the top of the game or at least close to it. It felt like I'd dictated large parts of the match, but physically I wasn't ready. Working on my fitness, so that I could mantain intensity right to the end, has been vital.

Another pivotal moment in my career was the first Davis Cup match I played in Israel, in 2005. I was just 17 years old and I'd never played in an atmosphere like that before. I played doubles with David Sherwood, a fellow Davis Cup debutant. We both fed off each other and won our match three sets to one. I was surprised by how well we played, despite being the underdogs and having the crowd against us. And I hadn't played a great deal of doubles up until then. I performed so well that the captain, Jeremy Bates, told me that if the tie had gone down to a deciding fifth match I would have played the singles. As I was so young at the time, that was a massive demonstration of faith in me. It was exciting because at that age people don't normally expect you to win and there was Jeremy saying that he thought I could.

Back when I was younger, I wish I had known the way the game was getting so physical. I wish I had trained more in the gym from a young age with that in mind, because once you start training you need to build up slowly and very gradually since your body is still developing. I was always quite powerful in my legs but my upper body was relatively weak and that's what I wish I'd worked on sooner.

My body was probably growing until I was about 19. I had to manage my knee condition, so I had to be patient for fear of injuring myself futher. What I do think is that I should have travelled with a trainer when I was younger and definitely had a physiotherapist. That way, I would have been made to stretch more, maybe even done more pilates from a younger age. Now it almost doesn't matter how much I do because it's really difficult to become more flexible. With all the training and matches, it doesn't leave me with much time for extra flexibility training. The focus has to be on maintaining what I have and making sure that I don't deteriorate, before I even start thinking about developing further.

So that's my one real learning from back in the early days of my career. But when you're younger, you're not really that interested in being professional. You'd rather focus on enjoying the game, so I can't quite bring myself to see that as a huge regret. Sometimes, things happen the way they do for a reason.

Maybe that was the case when I didn't make it to the French Open this year. Sometimes you have to know when to pick your battles, and I knew I wasn't going to win that one. In Madrid, I played both Florian Mayer and Gilles Simon at night and then another late one against Tomáš Berdych. The Berdych game finished at 2.30am and it took an awful lot of time afterwards with the physiotherapists and ice baths to get me feeling anywhere near normal. I noticed that my back was starting to get pretty sore during the long matches and in the one against Berdych it felt like it was getting a good deal worse.

I sat down with the guys after that match and we discussed the possibility of going on to play in the next tournament, the Rome Masters. I decided to take three days off beforehand and then hit some balls to see how my back responded. Unfortunately, that didn't work and in the match against Marcel Granollers on my 26th birthday it was really bad again. So bad, in fact, that I found I couldn't play through the pain. As well as the trouble I was in with my back, the weather was awful. There were gusty winds and both of us made a lot of mistakes. More importantly, I wasn't moving well. Marcel has known me from a young age and he didn't know what was happening with me. If you're making your opponent feel uncomfortable because of the way you're playing tennis, then that's fine, but if he's uncomfortable because you're clearly in pain, then that's something else.

I lost the first set 6–3, but despite the feeling that all the bones in my spine were slowly fusing together, I came back from 4–1 down to force a tie-break in the second. The guys had been telling me to stop a few games earlier and after I won that set I realised I wasn't enjoying myself but, worse than that, I could end up doing myself some real damage. With my back getting worse with each game, the score was becoming pretty irrelevant. My health was more important and I didn't want to play another set in agony. I decided to stop. I'd only previously pulled out of one ATP Tour match in about 500 I had played during my career. Oddly, the other time was five years before to the day, on my birthday, in Hamburg when I tore a wrist tendon.

Every player would rather lose the match a nd leave the court that way, but it wasn't to be and I flew home.

When I got to London, I saw a huge range of

doctors. There were two specialist back surgeons that I spoke to and another guy over in the US. I had some scans and then went through all of the medical procedures. We went to see Mark Bender and he examined my back and suggested some treatments to try to make it easier. But I hadn't been able to train properly during Madrid and Mark told me that I'd have to take a week to ten days off training to allow it to settle down properly and start a course of anti-inflammatories.

During that time I was struggling just to get up and down stairs, and trying to play what was potentially a series of five-set matches on clay wouldn't help my recovery. I'd played a significant number of Slams in a row and made the final of Wimbledon, the US Open and the Australian Open. It's not often a player has the opportunity to play in four Grand Slam finals in a row, so not competing at Roland Garros felt like a big decision. I know that next year, I need to manage that whole process better and accept that the clay season means a lot of wear and tear on my back in particular.

So for me, it felt like there was no point in going to the French just to be there. There was no chance of me doing anything in the tournament and I'm not interested in turning up just to say I managed to play a couple of matches. That's when we took the decision to drop out. After that, the focus shifted to what I could do to give myself the best chance of winning Wimbledon. The answer was to take the right amount of time off and then start training, hard, on grass.

7

CHAPTER 7

On the first day of the 2013 French Open, I was already on the grass. The weather was so cold in Paris that it would have done my back no good at all to compete there. Instead I was at Queen's Club, working on my routines, away from everyone bar my team and the odd photographer. I could go about my business quietly.

I've always felt welcome at Queen's and have been pretty successful there, but the premature end of my clay-court season meant this year's tournament was particularly important to me. If I hadn't got through a few preparatory matches, Wimbledon would have been really tricky on the back of six weeks with so little competitive tennis. That intensified the pressure. And my first opponent was Frenchman Nicolas Mahut, a seriously good grass-court player, who I had lost to in the opening round the previous year. I knew I had to make sure I was spot-on in terms of attitude and preparation.

When you start playing on grass again after clay, it's easier to serve well. At least, it seems that way. Even if you are not serving great, you get more from the ball off the surface. The return is tricky, though, because of the way the ball comes through compared with the clay. Then there are the adjustments that need to be made to deal with the different bounce on grass once the rally is underway. It's a lot lower, so you tend to get quite stiff in your back and your glutes. That's one of the reasons why the slice is a very important shot on the grass. You get rewarded with it more than you do on hard courts or clay. There are very few guys on the tour who can generate much pace with that shot on grass because they are used to the ball being up around the hips and shoulders. You can really put an opponent under a great deal of pressure with a good slice, so it's something I practise a lot. You just have to be careful not to overplay it, because you can end up doing quite a lot of running.

The extra grass-court practice seemed to help me this year at Queen's. It went as well as I could have hoped. I got in five good matches and took care of business without many difficulties. I got myself in a great position in every set of every match that I played, which was pleasing. Yes, there were tight sets against Benjamin Becker and Jo-Wilfried Tsonga, and I lost the first set in the final to Marin Čilić, the title-holder, but I felt good about lots of things with my game. I made some bad mistakes when I was up in the first set against Čilić, but I kept going for it. I was willing to take chances and felt like I was dictating a good many of the points.

I created loads of chances, and with a few more matches and a few more days' practice, I believed I would do a better job converting them at Wimbledon and would hope to eliminate the little slip-ups.

●　●　●

Earlier in the year I had agreed to do a BBC documentary that was going to be aired on the day before Wimbledon. I was worried it might be intrusive and I wasn't sure I wanted to do it. I met with the people from the BBC but still I wasn't tempted. None of the other guys in my coaching team were particularly keen either.

My lack of enthusiasm was based on shows like *Keeping up with the Kardashians*. I don't want to be waking up in the morning with a camera in my face and following me until last thing at night. I had a lot of trouble getting that thought out of my head.

Eventually I was persuaded because the BBC said they wouldn't take up too much time. They would get what they needed and leave – it's not like they would be following me around for weeks or coming to restaurants with me.

They came over for training in Miami and filmed for a couple of days and we agreed that if I didn't like the process and thought it was too much, then we could leave it. If it was OK, then we could proceed with it.

Actually it was easy, a good experience. Sue Barker was there, which helped because I know her well. I felt comfortable around her and didn't feel like she was digging to extract anything controversial or dodgy. I trust her.

Since it was aired, quite a few of the players, coaches and other people on the tour have come up and said they enjoyed it. Most of them had no idea about what had happened to me when I was younger. The general reaction was positive but it didn't have any effect on me going into Wimbledon. It might have changed the perceptions of other people about me, but it didn't change the way I felt about myself.

Having won the Olympic gold medal and the US Open the previous year, I expected to go into Wimbledon with a bit more confidence, but the feelings of nervousness and stress were still the same. Maybe after the US Open, I felt that playing a Slam wouldn't be the same arduous challenge anymore because I had won one, but for 99 per cent of the British population Wimbledon is the only one that really counts for the British players. I couldn't change that. I felt that pressure.

Getting the first win under the belt can be the trickiest at Wimbledon. I am always nervous before the opening match because the court plays differently for a couple of days; it is extremely green and tricky underfoot. So I was very pleased to put in a decent first-round performance against Benjamin Becker of Germany.

Elsewhere, Rafael Nadal went out in the first round to Steve Darcis of Belgium and Roger Federer was beaten in the second round by Sergiy Stakhovsky from Ukraine (the guy I had beaten in the US Open junior final in 2004). Both Rafa and Roger were in my half of the draw and as soon as they were out, all the media talk about how tough it was going to be for me suddenly turned. 'This is Andy's Wimbledon to win.' 'If he doesn't get to the final it will be a catastrophe.' That's why I never get obsessed with draws. But it is hard to block out that sort of talk and avoid complacency.

The fact that a lot of players were slipping and sliding on the courts in difficult conditions was also a concern. Against Lu Yen-hsun in the second round, I didn't feel comfortable at all. My movement was stiff and tentative. I was also playing on No.1 Court which plays a little differently to Centre Court so I wasn't settled. I felt anxious throughout, but managed to get through in straight sets.

The win set up a third round meeting with Tommy Robredo of Spain, the number 32 seed and a very fine player. We played under the roof on Centre Court which changes the conditions somewhat. It gives the court slightly different characteristics, which was something I needed to use to my advantage. I think I did a good job; it was my best match of the tournament.

Afterwards, I was asked again about the fact that

Roger and Rafa were gone from the event. What was I supposed to say? I just needed to retain my professional approach, play point by point and keep my head down. What was happening to other players really didn't affect me at all, even if it was getting some other people very hot under the collar.

● ● ●

Saturday afternoon brought some light relief as I got the opportunity to meet again some of my fellow Team GB Olympians, who had been invited into the Royal Box for the day. It was great to see some familiar faces, all decked out in their best. The Club asked if I would show my face in the box, so after a quick switch of clothes from my practice gear into a suit and tie (not my usual attire), I walked out to an ovation that was one of the most profound of my life. These are not the kind of occasions I particularly relish – I don't know quite what to do or say, but everyone wanted to shake hands, have their pictures taken, say a few encouraging words. That was special for me. My spirits were rising all the time.

● ● ●

On Monday, I felt really good in defeating the Russian, Mikhail Youzhny, in straight sets. My quarter-final opponent would be Fernando Verdasco of Spain, a left-hander, the first time I had played one since Feliciano López in the third round of the 2012 US Open.

It might not be easy for the layman to understand why, but playing lefties is very different because of their variety of spins and angles. And when Verdasco is having a good serving day – as he was this time – he is a daunting challenge.

I actually feel good against left-handers – they tend to hit it where I like to take the ball – but if they have an incredible day, there isn't much anyone can do. Verdasco served unbelievably and also started off returning especially well. I was playing average, solid stuff, not doing much of anything special. But when his level dropped I raised my game. He started to make some mistakes, got a little nervous, stopped serving as well and that was it. Seems simple, but that is the way it felt to me. It was a matter of waiting for my opportunity, sensing it and taking it when it came.

Even though it was a five-setter, there was not too much running involved – only three kilometres over three-and-a-half hours. Many of the points were quick ones. After the match, I was more mentally than physically tired. The whole affair was really draining and emotional. Often guys come back from two sets to love down and end up losing that fifth set because it is hard to keep that concentration and not have a dip for a few games. Luckily I didn't do that in the fifth and it was great to know I could come back to win without playing my best tennis.

Sir Alex Ferguson was watching the match from the Royal Box. I spoke to him for 20 minutes afterwards. He's the greatest football manager of all time. He has messaged me a few times before and during tournaments since we met at the US Open. He's been through all the pressures I face and understands how to block certain things out, especially the media attention, and concentrate on things that you can do something about. What anyone else says and does is largely irrelevant. You have to be true to yourself.

A lot of the time we were speaking about things other than tennis, but I often pick up one word, one gesture, one nugget and it can be golden. Experience is so important in sport and there is no one in the world who has more experience than Sir Alex of operating at the top level. He knows what can go wrong, the things you can and can't control, and the best way to go about giving yourself the opportunity to win. He says you need to get your tactics right, but you need a bit of luck as well. Sometimes luck doesn't go with you and you can lose. But there are things that are totally in your control, like concentration and focus, and if you get those right, you make yourself extremely difficult to beat. It must have been very special to have played for him.

I knew Sir Alex was there from the start of the match. I do spot people behind my opponent when he's tossing the ball up to serve. I have learned now not to think about who is there and who isn't, otherwise it can be a distraction. I am confident enough in my own ability to know that I can do this myself. But to have a full crowd on your side, that is something exceptional.

●　　●　　●

In the semi-finals, I was drawn to play Jerzy Janowicz, of Poland. He had been one of the stories at the end of 2012, racing through the field at the Paris Masters indoor event to reach the final and his ranking shot up as a consequence. He beat me in that tournament – I had a match point, but didn't follow through with a shot when I had a chance.

No one could predict how Janowicz would feel playing in his first Grand Slam semi-final. I know from experience that you feel so close to a final, but it also seems a huge distance away.

The prelude to our semi-final was a classic between Novak Djokovic and Juan Martín del Potro, lasting four hours and 43 minutes, which contained some amazing tennis. It meant that the shadows were lengthening when we stepped out at 6.15pm. I just hoped the light would hold.

My opponent hit a 139-mph ace in his first service game, a statement of intent. Against someone like Janowicz it is important to let them know you mean business, that whatever they do, you are right in there with them, not prepared to give an inch.

I lost the first set on a tie-break. It was clumsy on my part but it was only one set. I broke his first service game in the second set. It was past eight o'clock and I could sense he was getting agitated by the gradually worsening light. It was perfectly playable but he kept on chuntering to the umpire about it. When I won the third set from 4–1 down, which he wasn't happy about (neither was I that I let him have such a lead), he was going at the umpire again. I didn't see Andrew Jarrett, the referee, walking on to the court, but I suddenly sensed his presence.

'We're going to close the roof,' he told me.

I just thought he had to be kidding. Just because Janowicz is moaning about the light, we close the roof? Why? I wanted him to explain the rules to me but, as far as I recall, all he said was, 'It's the fairest thing to do . . . I've decided to close it.'

It was all rather chaotic, but we all trooped off court.

Back in the locker room, Janowicz was soon on his mobile phone, which was pretty hilarious when I come to think about it. It wasn't a quiet conversation either, he was pretty agitated. I just sat down with my team, had a shower, and got ready to come back out to play. Anyone would be a little angry at the circumstances. I had the momentum and the light was good enough to play. It was 8.40pm, hardly night-time at that time of the year. There was at least half an hour of playable light left.

But I knew I had to put that grievance behind

me. I had a job to finish. I wanted to win the match and win it now. And I was pleased with how quickly I settled down when we went back out on court. I played a really good fourth set.

And so I was into the Wimbledon final again, against Novak. It was a match-up I was beginning to relish.

● ● ●

In the Olympics if you lose the final, you still get a silver medal. A runner-up trophy at a Slam doesn't really compare with a silver medal. In the Wimbledon final, you have everything to gain and everything to lose at the same time. I had come through that semi-final against Janowicz and I knew I had a great chance of winning the final.

I was OK until the last 30 minutes before the match and then the nerves hit me again. Everyone else in my team was nervous as well. I'm sure Novak, Rafa and Roger and their teams were nervous but the knowledge that they'd won Wimbledon before must have helped. Last year I lost and I did think that I might never get another chance to do it. For me, someone who has never won it before, and my support team, the nervousness is heightened. And that's before you even think about it being my home Grand Slam and the extra expectation that entails.

It means the world to a lot of people, and that was apparent within my team in the hours before the match.

My strength and conditioning coach Matt Little was doing ball feeds, where he tosses balls from one side to the other to get my eye in, and he was throwing the ball all over the place. He couldn't keep one straight and it was making him anxious.

Ivan was on the practice court talking total nonsense – about the colour of the grass, about how the mud on the court is like part of this golf course he played recently. Anything.

Dani wasn't hitting the ball well at all as we warmed up. He was framing a lot of shots. Everyone was tight.

Looking back, it was a pretty poor preparation but I understand why. I would have been the same as them in their position. In some ways you want the match just to hurry up and arrive and yet in other ways you want to keep pushing it away.

Then, finally, there is the walk to Centre Court. The one thing that helped me there is that I've walked through that corridor so many times. As soon as I started the walk, I felt better. It didn't feel uncomfortable, the nerves eased. I know those hallways. I have sat on Centre Court, I have played numerous matches out there. I felt even better than the previous year. Walking to the court I could see people out of the window. People going up to the Hill, looking at their tickets, rushing to take their places. They looked happy. So I felt I should be, too.

The beginning of any match is really important, and even more so in a Grand Slam final. Statistics show that if you win the first set in a Slam final, you are much more likely to go on and win the match. And this time, I had three break points in the first game. I wanted to get that break from 0-40, I was hitting the ball well from the back of the court, but I didn't quite make it.

The best players in the world hit the ball that little bit cleaner and it comes off the racket with a sweeter sound. That takes time to adjust to sometimes, and Novak Djokovic was a step up from my semi-final opponent. Janowicz hits the ball hard, but not always out of the middle of the racket. He will hit a clean winner and the next one hits the back stop full pitch: that unexpected quality is unnerving. Novak is different. There is a predictable solidity about him. You know the ball is going to keep coming up the middle, there will be long rallies and if your game is not quite good enough you will be doing a lot of running as well.

It was so hot on the court during the final that I was using ice towels from very early on. I train in hot conditions but I had been back in the UK for six weeks and it hadn't been anywhere near that hot. In Madrid it was really cool and I played in the evening, three matches in succession. On the day I played Marcel Granollers in Rome it was windy and blustery. In the early stages of the Wimbledon final, I felt I couldn't breathe after the long points.

The final was much as I expected it, full of deep-hitting, energy-sapping rallies, Novak striking the ball out of the middle, and both of us looking for that essence of authority. Winning the first set was going to be critical and, after I couldn't convert any of my chances in the first game, I broke in the third with a backhand down the line, wrong-footing him. We had played 20 tortuous minutes and it was only 2-1. Then, in game four, I had three break points and took advantage of the second.

I immediately had Novak on the back foot on his serve again, earning three break points and taking the second. I hung on to my advantage this time, and when I eventually served out the set to love, I felt a rush. I had played the perfect service game and pretty much a perfect set.

I did get a bit defensive at the start of the second set and Novak pushed out to a 4-1 lead. At 4-2, I had two break points, but he won three in a row for advantage. I hung around in another long rally, broke his next serve and he double-faulted the game away. 4-3.

Four games to three became 4-4 and 5-5. At 15-all in the eleventh game, Novak got involved in a dispute with umpire Mohamed Lahyani about a baseline call – Novak thought the ball was out but there was no call and Hawk-Eye, so I'm told, said it was good. I had two break points and on the second, he netted. For the second time, I served out to love, this time finishing the set with an ace. Two sets to love up. A nice cushion but the job was nowhere near finished.

I have started to look at my opponents a lot more these days to see if I can gauge if they are tired or not, but it is usually a lot harder to read Novak than others. One minute you think he is tired and then the next few points he is sliding around the court. His movement is incredible and his endurance is the best on the tour right now. In this final, though, I sensed that he was tired after long rallies, even though I was always expecting him to recover. I could have been wrong because I had never won this title before. Maybe I wanted it that little bit more and was willing to go that little bit further than before to beat him.

I'd had to cover a lot of the court and by the beginning of the third set, I was feeling quite jaded. It had been a physical match and the nerves took quite a lot out of me as well.

At least the finishing line was in sight. I imagine it's the same as when you reach the last kilometre of a marathon and you feel much better than you did five kilometres out because you know the end is close. In the same way, it is a lot easier to chase the balls down when you are only one set away from finishing the match rather than another two-and-a-half sets, which is what it was looking like at 4–1 down 15 minutes previously. I was now in a position where I could really put the pressure on and try to close out the match.

These are the moments when you hope the years of work on the practice court will come into their own. Thankfully for me, my movement hasn't been something I've had to work on too much, but you have to be able to repeat those moves over and over again. That isn't enough, though. I don't always say it to the guys, but the reality is that having the movement to get to the ball doesn't matter if you can't execute the shot when you do. That's what separates the best from the rest. A lot of guys are physically strong but in those crucial moments you need to be able to execute the right shots with skill and accuracy. That comes from years of playing matches and, obviously, for a long period of my career I wasn't necessarily choosing or executing the right shots. But this day I definitely did.

I felt I was beginning to read Novak's intentions, even though I went from 2-0 up to 4-2 down in the third. I broke back, setting it up with a swinging forehand and he missed his backhand long. Then I held for four-all, with another of those running forehands to a backhand drop shot.

In the next game at 15-all, again I had to cover some ground. Novak played a drop shot, I could only flick it back, he played a lob, but I had the time to spin round and give chase and got enough of a racket on it to fire the ball at him before he could react. 15-30.

I suppose the next point was one of the most crucial. Novak struck a very solid forehand into my forehand corner which meant a scramble and a forehand 'get'. He swept his backhand deep into the opposite corner, which I managed to get back as well, this time with interest. He could only play an off-balance backhand volley and I had read it, moving up the court for a forehand winner.

An explosion of noise. The crowd was right in my head now. I could sense their support, their desire, their drive. I wanted to get them over the line. I was blowing hard, but so was Novak. When he netted a forehand on the next point, I remember him walking back to the chair and looking at him for a split-second. He kicked out at his racket bag. He was suffering. I was about to serve for Wimbledon.

● ● ●

A few fraught minutes (and deuces) later, the title was mine. In the celebrations after Novak's decisive netted backhand, I was aware that people had started to come onto the court. When I finally sat down, I saw Andrew Jarrett coming over.

'Have I got enough time to go to my family and friends?' I asked.

'You need to be quick.'

I climbed up to the players' box and went to Ivan first. He was sitting next to Novak's team. It wasn't a conscious decision to seek him out, but it was fitting that he was the first person I saw.

I've no idea if Ivan said anything to me or not. Two things I do recall: my uncle, Neil, was sitting a few rows back and he was so desperate to high-five me that he reached forward and stuck his armpit right in Sir Chris Hoy's face. Then, of course, I hadn't seen my mum and someone shouted, 'Your mum, your mum', so I went back and gave her a hug. I can't remember very much about what was said on the court after the trophy presentation. When you watch award shows, people speak for 15 minutes and they play the *Jaws* theme when they want them off the stage, but at Wimbledon it is controlled. I had to answer the questions asked of me and I think I did OK.

Everything was so hectic in the hours after we came off court, but being allowed to stand on the members' balcony with the trophy is something I will never forget. Just seeing all those happy people – happy for me, happy for themselves, happy for the nation. Just all incredibly supportive.

I had to change into my best suit for the Champions' Dinner. The menu wasn't really my kind of thing – small, posh plates of food – but it was pretty good, actually. The cool thing was to share the moment with the people there, the tennis family. Lots of past winners attended the dinner, like Rod Laver and Margaret Court, legends who have won so many titles and done so much for tennis.

I went up on stage to say a few words, but because of the other people there, I didn't feel as if I stood out. It is humbling to be among players who have won so much, but also nice to feel that I belong in that company.

The next day was frantic, too: more press, a trip to Lambeth to hit with some kids for a tennis promotion and then another change into a suit for a visit to No.10 Downing Street. I was standing outside for pictures and heard the door open and someone clap his hands. It was the Prime Minister. David Cameron is a big tennis fan and plays quite frequently. It was nice to have that recognition for what I'd achieved, but more so because my mum and dad were there. I could see they were very proud to see their son having a reception at Downing Street, thinking: 'My boy is all grown up now'.

8

CHAPTER 8

Life so far? It's been part adventure, part journey. There have been moments when I've felt the most intense joy imaginable, and moments of utter despair. There have been crucial wins and then defeats that come just when you think you've turned a corner. But the most important thing through it all is that I've made really, really close friends. These are people who I know will stay with me for the rest of my life because they were there for me right from the start and who are at the heart of my tennis journey. Even the people who joined along the way have all taught me different things about myself and the game. If it doesn't sound completely pretentious, they've taught me about life as well.

One of the main lessons I've learned is that the person you end up becoming has its roots in where you grew up and how you choose to live after that. And that the people who taught me right from wrong and shared their values with me, have shaped me for the rest of my life. That's my mum and dad.

People see me play and they talk about moments in a game where they think that I got lucky. What they don't see is all the hard work I put in on the training courts to get there in the first place. Where I did get lucky, though, was with my parents.

My brother Jamie and I started playing pretty much any sport we could think of from a young age. We loved being active and testing ourselves against each other, trying to see who was the best and who got bragging rights. Until the next time we played, anyway, when it'd start all over again. That's why it was great that both of my parents were so active and that they wanted to be active with us. They had full-time jobs, with my dad working from nine to five and my mum coaching tennis in various places. At the end of a long day, they might have wanted to sit down in front of the TV rather than take Jamie and me to tennis, or golf or football. They did take us, though, for everything from scuffles on the five-a-side pitch to some of our early tennis competitions. One of the things I know for certain is that neither of us would be where we are if they hadn't made the sacrifices they did.

One of the things we took for granted was that we didn't really do holidays. Well, we didn't really do them in the same way that most families seemed to. While the kids in our class were talking about going to Spain or somewhere like that, we never really went abroad. Maybe we went once, on a camping holiday, but it can't have been that great because I can only just about remember it. For the rest of the time we went to Center Parcs. It's not the most glamorous place in the world, but we used to absolutely love it. We'd go swimming, enter the five-a-side football tournament, play tennis. You name it, we were either doing it already or putting our names down for it. I guess that as a family we didn't really do lying on a beach.

My dad still plays five-a-side and golf a lot, which gives you an idea of what he was like when Jamie and me were growing up. As to my mum, she still loves coaching kids. It's one of those things that has never left her. The thing about Mum is that she wants to be on the court as much as she can, working with kids who are new to the sport, or ones who are starting to show potential. It doesn't matter to her. That's why I find it weird when people say that she's too pushy. She's unbelievably competitive and hates losing, which is probably where I get it from, but there's one thing that is worse for her, and that's not giving your best, no matter what you're doing. I can remember playing in a handicap mixed doubles event with her in North Berwick and I was probably about ten or eleven. That didn't stop Mum from having a right old swear and, like I say, that's something I can see in me as well.

We were lucky to have had parents like that, but we got lucky with our grandparents as well. They were there to help a lot, too, picking us up from school and taking us around to all the events. That's more of a big deal than it sounds, because there were no tournaments in Scotland. At the weekends, they'd drive us for five or six hours to England to play in small tournaments and then get us home again. There must have been times when they were exhausted at all the driving they had to do, but they never showed it or made us feel guilty. Whatever we wanted to do and wherever we wanted to play, they were there for us and that was massively important.

This might sound cheesy, but it's not really about

winning or losing for our family. They want Jamie and me to be OK; they want us to push ourselves, but within our limits. And if there's ever been signs that we wanted to stop, they've understood, whether it was us just lashing out or something more serious. You need that kind of support and I'm really glad of it.

Jamie went to an LTA academy in Cambridge when he was 12 and had a really bad experience that I think damaged his game. That was a massive backwards step in his development. He went from being one of the best in Europe for his age to really struggling in less than six months. It badly affected his confidence and for all the battles we'd had when we were young about who was the best, it was pretty shocking. When he came back, we could see what effect it had on him, so for my parents then to allow me to go off to Spain was a very important decision. Again, it shows that I was lucky with my parents. Really lucky. It would have been easy for them to see what had happened to Jamie and say, 'There's no way you're going', but they had faith in me and what I was trying to do. They let me go and, in the end, it turned out to be one of the key moments in my development as a player.

To be honest, going to the Academia Sánchez Casal in Spain was a big decision for me as well. Like most people who are growing up and testing their limits, I think I'd got to a point where I needed to be more independent, and more importantly, to work the way that I felt would be best for me. Maybe that sounds a bit arrogant, but sometimes that's just how you have to be. You could probably call it single-minded, but if you want to compete at the highest level, then that's how you have to be. Going away from home was extremely hard because I left behind everything that I knew. There were days when I was fighting my own homesickness, but I'm glad, really glad, that I stuck with it. There was another part of it as well. I pretty much lost any taste I might ever have had for alcohol. There was one night when I did some really stupid stuff that there's no way I'm going to write about here. The important thing is that I can't stand the taste of it, which is probably just as well.

● ● ●

One of the images from 2013 that I really cherish is that of my parents at the Wimbledon Champions'

Dinner. Mum and Dad are separated, but there they were, Mum, Dad and Dad's girlfriend, Samantha Watson, all chatting together, really happy. It was a wonderful night for me as well, for obvious reasons, and especially after all the heartbreak of the year before. To win the tournament in front of them, as well as all the other members of my family who had helped me along the way, was truly special. It's the moment when all the help of my parents and grand-parents driving me to junior tournaments, and the big decisions I made like going to Spain, really paid off. I wanted to thank them, and also all of the people who work with me. There's no way I could have done it by myself.

People often comment on the amount of people you have travelling with you, like it's an entourage or something. That's not how it works. Everyone has to justify their place, whether they're giving me the emotional support that I need or keeping me fit. Right at the heart of it all is my girlfriend, Kim.

I first met her at the US Open in 2005. She was on holiday with her dad Nigel who was coaching Daniela Hantuchová on the WTA Tour, so she under-stands tennis and the pressures that it puts on you, which helps a huge amount. To an outsider – and to me sometimes — it seems like a crazy sport and she understands that. Her dad also had a coaching job at the LTA and with individual players on the tour, and that all helps.

Kim was there in 2006 in San José when I won my first event which felt really important. It was all really innocent back then when I was just 19, but it was also hard to have a long-distance relationship. You're in these huge cities meeting new people all the time and it'd be easy to get your head turned. But Kim's always been there for me. She really cares about me and helps with so many things. She always has. That's why we have such a great relationship now.

One of the most important things about our relationship is that I have a lot of fun with Kim away from the courts, which takes all of the pressure off. Kim also understands when I need to be by myself and when I need companionship, which might sound like it isn't much, but it's really funda-mental as she's the person I spend most of my time with. Whether it's at an event or when we're at home, she's there when I go to bed and when I wake up. Kim sees all of the emotions when I win or lose a match, she can tell how I am really feeling and understands me.

When you are around the five guys in my immediate team for much of the time, it is normal that everyone wants to spark off each other and compete with each other. There's a lot of testosterone around. But away from that, Kim is the one who has to deal with all my different emotions which are very personal to me. And she is also very savvy about people. Kim can see which of them are trying to leech onto me, or who might want to be near me for their benefit rather than mine. That's not because of what I've done in tennis, but because of who they think I am and what I can do for them. A lot of times I'll hear from people who want to do deals with me, and that can make me feel a little vulnerable. Do I drop my guard and let them in, or do I feel wary about them for a reason? She gets all of that.

We do like a lot of the same things. Both of us like travelling, we don't get homesick and we both love dogs. When we got the second dog, that felt like a big commitment for both of us because one dog takes some looking after, but having two doubles that and adds a bit extra. It's not the same as having kids – or at least I don't think it is – but that's sometimes what it feels like.

I can see myself having a family one day. I imagine

it's something that most people would like to do if they get the chance, but I know it's tough to bring up kids. It is something that I'm starting to think about because Kim and I have been together for eight years. Added to that, I'm probably just past the halfway point of my playing career, so part of me is starting to think about what happens to me after I've finished playing, and what I do next. But that's all about the timing, too, and where I am when the day comes. I know Roger Federer has spoken about how keen he was to have his kids see him play. That's not something I'm particularly desperate for and I suppose it won't be happening anytime soon, but when I'm done playing, yes, I would like to start a family and try to be a good father. That's important to me.

● ● ●

Along with Kim, there's Dani Vallverdu. Every team needs a constant, a cornerstone. And he's mine. The way I have had things set up in the group is that there have been physical trainers who come in just for a few weeks, and in recent months I have worked with a range of different physiotherapists. Ivan would come for a few weeks at the important times but Dani has

Not the predominantly white of the Wimbledon Championships but I really felt comfortable in the blue kit of Team GB during the 2012 Olympics.

(Top) Is it relief or disbelief? Whatever the emotion, winning the US Open, my first Grand Slam, was a massive accomplishment. (Bottom) A chance to plant a smacker on the trophy.

(Top) With Mum, Dani Vallverdu, Andy Ireland and Jez Green at the UK Ambassador's residence. What a special moment to share.

(Bottom) Sharing another victory, this time it's my Olympic Gold with some kids in Dunblane. They had produced some great drawings to celebrate my success. It brought back a lot of memories.

(Top) It is amazing to think of myself as part of this company. Alongside Novak, Roger and Rafa at the Barclays ATP World Tour Finals, recognising Roger's immense achievements.

(Bottom) The first time I played Roger, at the final of the Thailand open in 2005. How we've both changed!

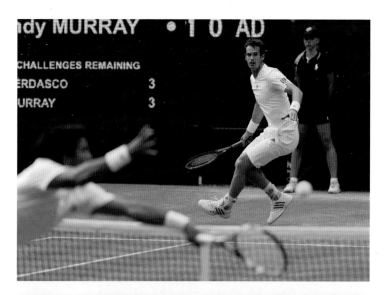

(Top) Fernando Verdasco at full stretch in our five-set quarter-final at Wimbledon 2013, which lasted three hours and 27 minutes. It was not so much a physical test as a mental one.

(Bottom) Pausing for reflecton in the latter stages of the final against Novak. One mistake can mean so much so you have to stay focused.

I really don't know what to think, what to do, where to go, how to respond. The enormity of what I have achieved is slowly beginning to skink in. I love looking at that scoreboard.

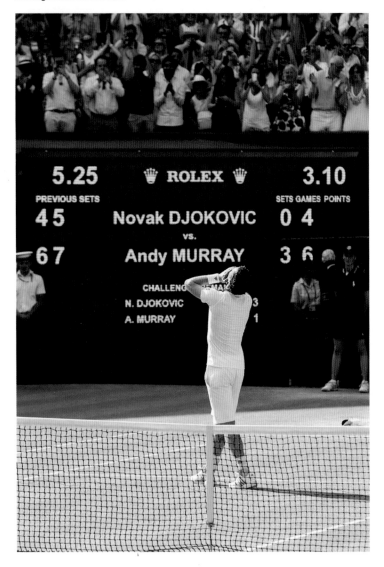

My body is drained of all emotion.
I am overcome. I'm the only one not
on my feet!

Finally, I manage to climb to the players' box to greet
as many people as I can. First is Ivan, who has done
so much for me but probably doesn't expect a hug.
And then, a kiss for Kim, who has seen her fair share of
the difficult moments and always wants the best for me.

This is one scene I had not expected. There didn't seem to be an inch of space to be had when I came out onto the members' balcony to show off the cup. Amazing scenes.

(Left) Another one of those 'Is this really happening to me?' moments. (Right) The joy of winning is etched on my face. Happy days.

been ever-present for the last three years and that consistency has been vital to my success. He is only 26 years old, but he's seriously well-organised and he's in charge of an awful lot more than just hitting balls with me. Not everyone knows what goes into a tennis player's day-to-day life, but it's very, very complicated.

For a start, there are 500 players looking for a practice court. You need to find the right people to practise with, and make sure you get to the right courts at the right time. You have to sort out the balls and make sure that the player you're working with doesn't forget anything. And at the end of it all you have to make sure that the whole team is where they should be and at the right time.

One of the qualities that they have to demonstrate is that they can follow instructions from someone like Ivan and make sure that you're doing all the right drills, because that's a vital part of your coaching.

If that makes it sound like Dani is just a robot, he isn't. He's a very independent voice with his own opinions about the way that things are set up, and I know how much Ivan appreciated what he did both for him and for me. Dani is the guy who works with me for 40 weeks per year. And those are full weeks, packed full of very, very hard work for both of us.

He takes care of the small details extremely well and all of those small details add up to a huge part of the overall picture. It's because of Dani's hard work that I never turn up for practice and find no one else is there. He checks the weather in advance to make sure we don't have a two-hour practice session scheduled when thunderstorms are forecast, and if there is he'll have an indoor court booked and a practice partner for me who with is happy to go indoors.

When you have a tournament coming up, whether it's Wimbledon, the US Open or one of the smaller tournaments, you need someone who is on top of all the details to allow you to focus solely on your game. Dani does all of that, but he also understands me. He's known me since I was 15 and can tell whether I'm genuinely upset or just having a bit of a moan. That can be during matches, when we're practising or elsewhere. He also knows when I'm moaning about something I don't really care about or if I'm nervous and so it's better not to engage me in conversation. Having someone around like him is vital.

Dani and I have a friend called Carlos Mier from Peru. I first met him when I went over to Spain and he, Dani and I have been best friends ever since. In the ten years I've known him, nothing has changed. Because of the way tennis works, it is difficult to have a very large group of friends. You spend so much time away that when you are at home you don't have time to see 20 different friends. It is a small group and the guys are very special to me. Carlos, Dani and I were attached at the hip at the Academy. We've been really good friends for a long time and he's a fun person to be around. Importantly, he couldn't care less that I've been successful. Of course he's happy for me, but it wouldn't matter to him if I was just a middle- or low-ranked player. He treats me exactly the same way and that's why I like him so much. It is me that matters to him, not what I've accomplished.

What Dani doesn't do is set my overall fitness regime. That's the responsibility of Jez Green and Matt Little. They are the two guys responsible for keeping me in the best shape that I can be. They run my programmes and they oversee my fitness regime. At the same time, they're there for me and that's the support I need so much.

I employed Jez a few years back. He had been around the game a long time and had developed an excellent reputation. Matt came on board a little later.

They communicate well with each other and know what I need in each different set of conditions. They share the responsibilities and I think that makes them enjoy the experience of working together. They appreciate how the game has developed, so they also know that they need to make me as strong as you need to be. That's why I'm out on the practice court and then go the gym afterwards even if my whole body is tired and sore. I'll be moaning about it and asking to stop and they have to hear all of that. They probably do feel a little responsible for my complaints, but they also know that I need to do the work if I want to have a chance of winning my next big tournament. They always say, 'Well, you'll be thanking us in 20 days' time,' which makes me groan at the time, but often they're right.

Maybe I could have employed a couple of guys who would let me take it easy when I say I'm too tired to continue, but that's just not how I need this to work, and they know that. I have an excellent relationship with both of them and they're really good friends, but they're honest with me. They'll push me and drive me to work harder, but also they don't make me push myself too hard when I don't need to. That's important and that knowledge only develops when you have a really good understanding of where the other person's comfort zones are and where their limits are. They can find me something to do, a way to work my way around any tiredness I might be feeling that stops training becoming too repetitive and dull.

The training is full on. It is specific. And most importantly, it works for me. I have done a lot of brutal sessions where I'm shattered by the end and I've trained in some really tough conditions. They have seen all of that and been with me through all of the losses, but lately they've been there for some of the special wins, too. Perhaps at times during the losses and setbacks, they doubted themselves and their training regime or doubted my ability to follow it through. I don't know. But to have been able to share these wins with them was great. Ivan knows what it takes, but he didn't sit and watch all my fitness sessions. I practise for two hours and then he leaves. Then it's over to the gym to work with Jez even though I'm already tired from practice. You can do it another way and try to cheat your way in life, but if you want to win tournaments and do things properly, you have to go through those sessions even when it hurts. They know that, and they're sympathetic to me, but they also know that I need to get these things done.

Mark Bender is another guy I've known for a long time. My back has been an issue for a little while and it's the main priority in terms of physiotherapy. It was Mark who gave a job to a guy called Andy Ireland when he opened his clinics, so they know each other really well, and then Andy started working with me, which I'm really grateful to Mark for.

Mark used to be the Davis Cup physiotherapist and I reminded him recently that he had told me off when I was 15, and had been brought into the team to get to know everyone. Jeremy Bates was the captain and brought me in for a tie in Austria. The team got a bad call in the doubles and I was booing, so Mark elbowed me and said, 'What do you think you're doing?' When I mentioned it to him recently he said that it sounded like a shitty thing for him to do, but I said I had learned my lesson and I've never done it since.

Johan De Beer, who worked with Tim Henman and has been on the staff at the LTA, has been helping me out a lot this year. I generally see a physiotherapist for 40 minutes before practice and then for anything up to an hour in the evenings. Fifty per cent of that time is spent on working my back. The exercises we do in the gym are designed specifically to give me more flexibility in certain areas and to strengthen others. It's injury-prevention work basically. I spend a lot of time on that, each day, every day and these are the things that those who don't know the game don't see. They think we go on the court and play, but the days before a Grand Slam championship are especially long. There's practice, up to 90 minutes of important remedial work, travelling, sponsor days and media requirements. The time soon adds up.

There have been many, many different influences on me, but one of the main ones was Leon Smith. I worked with him from the age of 12 until I was 17 and it was a different sort of relationship between player and coach at that time. He made me enjoy my tennis and I loved being with him at tournaments and being away from home. Leon was really young and we were both inexperienced but it somehow made it even more of an adventure. I recall when I first hurt my knee and he was there, advising me the best he could. It got worse and worse over time and I probably didn't have the best advice from some of the other people. I was told that it was growing pains, but it got to the point where I couldn't walk.

I lost a match 6-0, 6-0 to Jan Masik of the Czech Republic in Gran Canaria and couldn't even bend my knee. There wasn't much in the way of medical expertise out there and I was just told to ice it and it'd soon get better. After the loss to Masik I didn't play a match for seven months and even then I had to retire. Every day, Leon would come to see me and spend time with me, listen to me and try to give as much good advice as he could. It wasn't as if he was a shoulder to cry on, but another young guy to confide in.

As a coach, Leon has improved immeasurably. He has learned more and more and gained loads of experience. But I think he is at his best when he runs his eye over young players. He experienced every stage of my development. He has the ability to identify players at under-12 and under-14 level who are going to excel. The Davis Cup results have been going in the right direction and you can tell how well the players respond to him by the results they've pulled out. Earlier this year against Russia in Coventry, Dan Evans and James Ward recovered from a couple of body-blow defeats on the first day and responded with victories over Dmitry Tursunov and Evgeny Donskoy, players who are ranked much higher than them. A lot of this is down to Leon's sound captaincy. He has this ability to say the right thing at the right time, to quietly analyse a match and he doesn't complicate things. The way he has grown into his new roles at the LTA has been really impressive, but I'm not too surprised.

●   ●   ●

When I think about all of my physios and all of the people who have worked on my game, I wish that when I was younger I'd taken better care of myself. Tennis is really tough now and your body starts to hurt, especially when you get to your mid-twenties. At 18, you don't feel anything. You recover quickly. But that's the age I was when I started on the tour and it's been eight years of hard, physical work. It all takes it out of you, especially the hard courts.

That's why I think they need to reduce the amount of time I play on the hard courts and perhaps have a longer grass season. The hard courts are very tough on your body and, when you get into your twenties, you can really feel that. The guys who played in past eras were wonderful players and tremendous athletes, but they were able to play their Grand Slams on grass. I wouldn't mind that at all. Tennis may not go down that route, but I'd love to see some more grass-court tournaments. I'm delighted there will be three weeks between the French Open and Wimbledon by 2015 – that's a brilliant move by the All England Club. There have been suggestions of trying to change some of the tournaments in the USA to green clay so you could potentially have Grand Slams on four different surfaces: red clay, green clay, grass and hard courts. That's not a bad idea, though I'll believe it when I see it. It does show that tennis is changing, but then I suppose it always has. If you'd told the guys with wooden rackets that we'd be playing with graphite composite rackets and striking the balls at speeds we do now, they'd have been amazed, but that's what makes it a great sport. It's always evolving, and as players, we're part of that journey, too.

CHAPTER 9

I felt different in the ten days or so after becoming the Wimbledon champion. I had more of a glow, walked a little bit taller and felt more self-confident because winning was a big accomplishment, something I had tried to do for such a long time. I was under so much pressure and so after conquering that task, I wanted to enjoy it.

Kim and I stayed in a hotel in London the first couple of nights after I won because there was so much to do. Then we went home and collapsed. We didn't leave the house for a couple of days, before heading off to the Bahamas for a holiday.

The first day, we went down to the beach and

played a bit of bat and ball. When we woke up the next morning, there were a load of text messages saying pictures of us were all over the internet. Both of us were like, 'We're not going to the beach anymore'. It was a shame because our hotel was right on the beach, but we didn't want to have our pictures taken. We waited until the last day at 7pm to walk on the beach and the same paparazzi guy was waiting there. I stared at him for 10 minutes while we were walking, he didn't take any pictures and then he left. I don't enjoy that intrusive side. I don't mind having pictures taken in the street or signing autographs, but being followed on your holiday is not my idea of fun.

● ● ●

Now I've had more time to reflect on my Wimbledon success, I hope that it will make a difference to how tennis is viewed in the country. I don't know if my win will inspire a new generation, but if it helps a little bit, I will feel as if I have kept my side of the bargain. It is now down to the people in charge to capitalise and to do the right things for the sport to move forward.

I am not saying me winning Wimbledon makes

any difference to a young British player on the tour, but it would be nice to think it could inspire the likes of Dan Evans and James Ward. Dan and James have done well since, and they might not have done that if I hadn't won Wimbledon, but if it has given them and other players in this country even one per cent more focus, a feeling of 'we can do it, too', that would be great. It would be really satisfying to make a difference to the future of British tennis. I'm happy to offer advice now, and when I have finished playing that is something I would like to help with.

I'm excited for the future. I'm looking forward to enjoying the rest of my career because I'll never play another game like that at Wimbledon. In some ways maybe that is a little sad, but for the most part I'm happy never to have to deal with that kind of expectation again. I think that should help me, but I have always played my best tennis when there has been additional pressure so you never know. I just want to try and achieve more. I will keep working hard and hope my body and health holds up for a few more years to give me an opportunity to do that.

Within a month of winning the Wimbledon Ladies' title, Marion Bartoli retired from the game, which shows that you can't take anything for granted.

In a way, it was a nice conclusion to Marion's career, and she will be remembered for it. In my case, becoming the first British man to win Wimbledon in 77 years, it doesn't matter what I do now because that is what I'll be remembered for.

I think it would have been an absolutely perfect ending if Marion hadn't played Cincinnati after Wimbledon, but maybe she needed confirmation that she didn't want to play anymore. Playing in front of a few hundred people in Cincinnati is not playing in front of a full house on Centre Court. And this is not meant as a slight, but she had reached her potential. She worked as hard as she could as an athlete and that is ultimately what you want to be known for. For Dan Evans, say, if his potential is the top 50 in the world and he gets there, that's all you can do. There aren't many people who can say they have given everything to the sport, fulfilled their potential and then called it a day.

In the case of Ivan Lendl, he used every ounce of his ability to reach the very top of the game as a player. Now, he has proved himself as a top coach. It isn't easy. The best players don't always make the best coaches. And Ivan did a great job with me but might not do so well if he moves on to someone else. There has to be a good fit, but one of the signs of a great coach is relating to everyone and adapting to a player's needs. He's been flexible, and he has learned more about the game. He hadn't followed tennis closely since his retirement, just the end of Grand Slams. He didn't know many of the current players and the game had changed. There are aspects of the modern game which have advanced, but also there are skills which players of his era did better, like volleying, because more players came to the net then.

Ivan has adapted well to being a coach and it's nice for him to be around people in the sport again. I think he's enjoyed that because he was away from the scene for a long time. He's got five daughters who he's raised so well; they all love their sports. I think he enjoyed being around Dani, treating him like a son in a way, and me similarly.

He made me learn more from losses than maybe I did in the past. I think he was always very honest with me, told me exactly what he thought. In tennis, it's not always that easy to do in a player/coach relationship. The player is often the one in charge and coaches are not always that comfortable with being brutally honest. With Ivan, it was simple: if I worked hard, he was happy, if I didn't, he was disappointed, and he'd tell me.

And when I lost matches, he wasn't necessarily negative. After the 2012 Wimbledon final he told me he was proud of the way I played because I went for it when I had chances. It was the first time I played like that in a Grand Slam final. He's altered my mentality slightly going into those sort of matches.

People think Ivan doesn't get too emotional, and that he doesn't usually say anything during matches but in the US Open and the Wimbledon final last year, he was really agitated. On those rare occasions when he started to show emotion, I picked up on it quite quickly. Watch the Wimbledon final again. I could tell he was nervous. It was nice for me to see that because he has been there and done everything. During the match he was getting up all the time, standing up at the change of ends, clapping, he was talking a lot to Dani. They didn't ever seem to stop talking.

I could see how important it was to him. For the first five rounds he didn't move, but this was the Wimbledon final, a stage he'd reached himself as a player. This was why he wanted to come back to tennis. He wanted to be the best coach he could be and it was nice to see him in a bit of a state in the final. I liked that.

He is pretty calm generally, though, and doesn't say much. Sometimes, I wanted to see a little more emotion, but he's worked over a lot of years to be able to disguise his emotions and that is part of his nature. That is him. You have to accept that. He would like me to show less emotion, too, and I have got better at it but, for me, it is still hard.

● ● ●

Everyone was saying before Wimbledon that it was a great time for the sport, an era of great matches and rivalries. A British man winning Wimbledon was one of the few things that was missing. To be able to change that is brilliant. It's been a feelgood news story, good for tennis in general, and I'm glad I've been a part of that.

Another change that happened before I won the Championship was that I became a full member of the All England Club. They had asked me a couple of years before and I'd declined. I wasn't being disrespectful, but I couldn't see myself using the facilities at the club. I didn't train there, I didn't practise there and I didn't think I'd hang out there. I also didn't want to feel obliged to come to functions because they had given me membership. This year, though, I sat down with Tim Henman, who is now on the management committee, and he said they had discussed it again. He reassured me that they wouldn't bug me to do anything, so I said, 'OK, let's do it.'

It's actually been great because it is always quiet there when I need some quiet. It is nice and relaxed; cool. Cooler still, now I'm the champion.

And now, inevitably, questions are asked about where to next. Am I satisfied? What about the next stage of my career?

The number-one ranking does not motivate me, it really isn't what I am all about. What drives me is winning the Grand Slams. Getting to number one would be nice, but my career has become about the Slams. That is not something I necessarily decided for myself. It originated from the expectations of the press and public, and years of being questioned about not winning them. When I had a chance to go to number one in the world a few years, the attitude seemed to be, 'Well if he gets there but hasn't won a Grand Slam, what does it matter?' If I didn't win one, I was a failure.

And I also know that even if I had won the Australian Open this year, I could have held the title there, Wimbledon, the US Open and the Olympics and still not been anywhere near world number one. So my motivation isn't to be the best player based on what a ranking system says, but to perform in Grand Slams. That's what I train for and that's what excites me.

On reflection, winning Wimbledon could be looked upon as the achievement of my life's work. It would be easy to say I've done what I set out to do and that nothing else will quite be the same again. In one way it won't – the achievement is there for all to see and for me to appreciate. I am perceived differently by others, even if I don't feel much different myself.

Maybe I shall never truly get my head around what I have done. I am supposed to be more relaxed and yet, at the US Open this year, I felt a little more tense, a bit uptight. The expectations had changed in another, subtle way, one that I hadn't expected. The stress of winning that last game at Wimbledon may have taken a toll. I didn't play as well as I would have wanted to in New York. It was tough. I lost in the quarter-finals to Stanislas Wawrinka of Switzerland, who is playing the best tennis of his life and was a deserving winner that day. I didn't feel myself there but my best form will come back, I am sure of that. And should reaching the quarter-finals of a Grand Slam tournament be regarded as a failure, anyway? I don't think so.

The tone of the press questions was different at the Open and yet I still felt a bit on edge. It is this eternal struggle to justify yourself, whatever you have done. Tennis is like that. Roger wins 17 Grand Slams and it is always, 'What next?'. The same is true for Rafa and for Novak. Novak brought in the Pole, Wojtek Fibak, who coached Ivan at an early stage in his career, to help him find that something extra. We never stand still.

Perhaps I won't be able to fully appreciate my achievements until the day I say, that's it, I've done all the work I could have done, there is nothing more for me to give. That won't be for some time yet. There is planning to be done for the future. I have set up my own company, 77, and I'm keen to get involved with sports stars of the future, maybe events, who knows? These are different times, and challenging, too. For me, the challenge never ends.

And a fantastic challenge I'm looking forward

to in 2014 is representing Great Britain in the World Group of the Davis Cup. We played a great match in Umag, Croatia, in September to gain promotion. There is a great sense of togetherness in the British camp. A lot of good people work for the game in this country at so many different levels and the Davis Cup is an opportunity for us all to show what it means to represent Britain. The sense is different from when you are out there on your own. I know I have the support from my box – that's a given – but this is right there, in your face, the whole time.

Leon Smith has done a great job as the captain, there is great respect all round and I love the camaraderie that team sports foster. I wanted to play on all three days of the Croatia tie and while I cannot say that will happen all the time, if I think it will help the team to do that and the captain agrees, I will.

I played Ivan Dodig in the first reverse singles in Croatia. On my third match point the crowd was so noisy after a call had gone against Ivan on the previous point. He felt the ball was in, I knew it was out, the umpire agreed but the crowd refused to let it drop. Well, I've served for the Wimbledon final now, and managed to get over the winning line, so I just smiled, served, played a really good point and we won the tie.

I've had some pretty wonderful experiences this year but that was right up there with them. The joy on everyone's face was a picture. I cherish those moments.

Of course it did make me pause and think about how I had felt on Centre Court a few weeks earlier. What if I hadn't won that tenth game of the third set? What if Novak Djokovic had taken one of his three break points and it had been level at 5-5? These are questions that may always be raised – I raise them myself from time to time – and yet none of us can know the answer. I won the final point of the Wimbledon final. I dropped my racket, flicked off my hat and punched the air. That sensation will never leave me.

I made a lot of people very happy that day. Not only my friends, my followers, my supporters, and the media, but, from what I have heard, people around the world who have never met me, don't know me, but have heard of my struggles and have been on my side. To know they are out there for me means so much.

Immediately after the Croatia tie, I decided that I finally needed to make sure my back was OK. I think it's important to give the body time to recover – we are on the tour for over 40 weeks of the year and there aren't many opportunities. All players pick up niggles and knocks, it's just about understanding and managing your body as best you can.

I had a minor operation, nothing too complicated. The most important thing for me now is doing the rehabilitation work. I've now got some time to rest and let my body recover before I head out to Miami to get myself ready for the new season. The last year or so has been incredible and maybe I haven't taken enough time to actually process and enjoy everything. I can't wait to be fit and ready for the new season and come back even stronger. The first thing I said when the anaesthetic wore off was 'Did I win?'

I have a lot more to give in my life but if I am remembered for 11 minutes on Centre Court at Wimbledon in 2013, it will be no bad thing. It was career-affirming and the match felt like my life in miniature. Free and easy at first, a stumble, another stumble, a recovery, another stumble, a recovery, run, run, run, sprint for it, make your choices, move, recover, pick your spot, stand tall, play the game, win the point. That is me, really.

Index

Playing Statistics

Complete results for all Grand Slam and Olympic tournaments in which Andy has reached the final.

Australian Open 2010
Round 1

Roger Federer (SUI) [1] beat Igor Andreev (RUS) 4-6 6-2 7-6 6-0
Victor Hanescu (ROU) beat Juan Ignacio Chela (ARG) 6-4 6-3 7-6
Stephane Robert (FRA) beat Potito Starace (ITA) 6-3 7-6 7-6
Albert Montanes (ESP) [31] beat Oscar Hernandez (ESP) 7-6 2-2
   (Hernandez retired)
Lleyton Hewitt (AUS) [22] beat Ricardo Hocevar (BRA) 6-1 6-2 6-3
Donald Young (USA) beat Christophe Rochus (BEL) 1-6 7-5 6-2 6-4
Marcos Baghdatis (CYP) beat Paolo Lorenzi (ITA) 6-2 6-4 6-4
David Ferrer (ESP) [17] beat Frederico Gil (POR) 6-0 6-0 2-0 *(Gil retired)*
Fernando Verdasco (ESP) [9] beat Carsten Ball (AUS) 6-7 7-6 7-5 6-2

Ivan Sergeyev (UKR) beat Dudi Sela (ISR) 6-3 7-6 4-6 7-6

Stefan Koubek (AUT) beat Rajeev Ram (USA) 6-3 3-6 7-5 1-6 3-6

Ivan Dodig (CRO) beat Juan Carlos Ferrero (ESP) [23] 2-6 1-6 6-4 6-1 6-1

Juan Monaco (ARG) [30] beat Ernests Gulbis (LAT) 6-3 7-6 6-1

Michael Llodra (FRA) beat Martin Vassallo Arguello (ARG) 6-3 7-5 6-4

Illya Marchenko (UKR) beat Carlos Moya (ESP) 7-6 7-5 6-3

Nikolay Davydenko (RUS) [6] beat Dieter Kindlmann (GER) 6-1 6-0 6-3

Novak Djokovic (SRB) [3] beat Daniel Gimeno-Traver (ESP) 7-5 6-3 6-2

Marco Chiudinelli (SUI) beat Marinko Matosevic (AUS) 7-6 7-6 4-6 6-3

Michael Berrer (GER) beat Kristof Vliegen (BEL) 6-1 6-2 6-1

Denis Istomin (UZB) beat Jeremy Chardy (FRA) [32] 6-2 6-2 6-0

Mikhail Youzhny (RUS) [20] beat Richard Gasquet (FRA) 6-7 4-6 7-6 7-6
  6-4

Jan Hajek (CZE) beat Robby Ginepri (USA) 7-6 7-5 6-1

Lukasz Kubot (POL) beat Mischa Zverev (GER) 6-3 6-3 6-3

Santiago Giraldo (COL) beat Tommy Robredo (ESP) [16] 6-4 6-2 6-2

Jo-Wilfried Tsonga (FRA) [10] beat Sergiy Stakhovsky (UKR) 6-3 6-4 6-4

Taylor Dent (USA) beat Fabio Fognini (ITA) 6-1 6-3 6-3

Janko Tipsarevic (SRB) beat Ryan Harrison (USA) 6-2 6-4 7-6

Tommy Haas (GER) [18] beat Simon Greul (GER) 6-7 6-4 6-2 6-1

Nicolas Almagro (ESP) [26] beat Xavier Malisse (BEL) 7-6 6-4 2-6 4-6 8-6

Benjamin Becker (GER) beat Grega Zemlja (SLO) 7-6 7-5 7-5

Alejandro Falla (COL) beat Marcos Daniel (BRA) 7-5 6-3 6-1

Marcel Granollers (ESP) beat Robin Soderling (SWE) [8] 5-7 2-6 6-4 6-4
  6-2

Andy Roddick (USA) [7] beat Thiemo de Bakker (NED) 6-1 6-4 6-4

Thomaz Bellucci (BRA) beat Teymuraz Gabashvili (RUS) 6-3 7-5 4-6 6-4

Feliciano Lopez (ESP) beat Pablo Cuevas (URU) 6-1 6-4 7-5

Rainer Schuettler (GER) beat Sam Querrey (USA) [25] 6-0 6-3 6-3

Tomas Berdych (CZE) [21] beat Robin Haase (NED) 6-0 6-3 6-3

Evgeny Korolev (KAZ) beat Daniel Brands (GER) 6-2 7-5 7-5

Marsel Ilhan (TUR) beat Sebastien Grosjean (FRA) 6-4 6-3 7-5

Fernando Gonzalez (CHI) [11] beat Olivier Rochus (BEL) 6-3 6-4 3-6 6-1

Marin Cilic (CRO) [14] beat Fabrice Santoro (FRA) 7-5 7-5 6-3

Bernard Tomic (AUS) beat Guillaume Rufin (FRA) 6-3 6-4 6-4

Igor Kunitsyn (RUS) beat Jose Acasuso (ARG) 6-1 2-6 6-4 6-2

Stanislas Wawrinka (SUI) [19] beat Guillermo Garcia-Lopez (ESP) 6-3 6-3
6-2

Viktor Troicki (SRB) [29] beat Nicolas Lapentti (ECU) 4-6 6-3 6-1 6-3

Florian Mayer (GER) beat Philipp Petzschner (GER) 0-6 2-6 6-4 6-2 6-2

James Blake (USA) beat Arnaud Clement (FRA) 7-5 7-5 6-2

Juan Martin Del Potro (ARG) [4] beat Michael Russell (USA) 6-4 6-4 3-6 6-2

Andy Murray (GBR) [5] beat Kevin Anderson (RSA) 6-1 6-1 6-2

Marc Gicquel (FRA) beat Simone Bolelli (ITA) 7-6 7-6 6-3

Jarkko Nieminen (FIN) beat Nick Lindahl (AUS) 6-2 7-5 6-4

Florent Serra (FRA) beat Jurgen Melzer (AUT) [28] 6-1 6-7 6-4 4-6 6-3

John Isner (USA) [33] beat Andreas Seppi (ITA) 6-3 6-3 3-6 5-7 6-4

Louk Sorensen (IRL) beat Yen-Hsun Lu (TPE) 6-4 3-6 6-2 6-1

Antonio Veic (CRO) beat Daniel Koellerer (AUT) 6-4 3-6 6-7 6-1 6-4

Gael Monfils (FRA) [12] beat Matthew Ebden (AUS) 6-4 6-4 6-4

Ivo Karlovic (CRO) beat Radek Stepanek (CZE) [13] 2-6 7-6 6-4 3-6 6-4

Julien Benneteau (FRA) beat David Guez (FRA) 0-6 6-4 7-6 7-6

Andrey Golubev (KAZ) beat Mardy Fish (USA) 6-2 1-6 6-3 6-3

Ivan Ljubicic (CRO) [24] beat Jason Kubler (AUS) 6-1 6-2 6-2

Philipp Kohlschreiber (GER) [27] beat Horacio Zeballos (ARG) 6-1 7-5 6-1

Wayne Odesnik (USA) beat Blaz Kavcic (SLO) 4-6 6-1 6-4 6-2

Lukas Lacko (SVK) beat Leonardo Mayer (ARG) 6-4 6-4 6-0

Rafael Nadal (ESP) [2] beat Peter Luczak (AUS) 7-6 6-1 6-4

Round 2

Roger Federer (SUI) [1] beat Victor Hanescu (ROU) 6-2 6-3 6-2

Albert Montanes (ESP) [31] beat Stephane Robert (FRA) 4-6 6-7 6-2 6-3 6-2

Lleyton Hewitt (AUS) [22] beat Donald Young (USA) 7-6 6-4 6-1

Marcos Baghdatis (CYP) beat David Ferrer (ESP) [17] 4-6 3-6 7-6 6-3 6-1

Fernando Verdasco (ESP) [9] beat Ivan Sergeyev (UKR) 6-1 6-2 6-2

Stefan Koubek (AUT) beat Ivan Dodig (CRO) 7-6 6-1 6-2

Juan Monaco (ARG) [30] beat Michael Llodra (FRA) 3-6 3-6 7-6 6-1 6-3

Nikolay Davydenko (RUS) [6] beat Illya Marchenko (UKR) 6-3 6-3 6-0

Novak Djokovic (SRB) [3] beat Marco Chiudinelli (SUI) 3-6 6-1 6-1 6-3

Denis Istomin (UZB) beat Michael Berrer (GER) 7-5 6-3 6-4

Mikhail Youzhny (RUS) [20] beat Jan Hajek (CZE) 6-2 6-1 6-1

Lukasz Kubot (POL) beat Santiago Giraldo (COL) 6-4 3-6 6-3 6-1

Jo-Wilfried Tsonga (FRA) [10] beat Taylor Dent (USA) 6-4 6-3 6-3

Tommy Haas (GER) [18] beat Janko Tipsarevic (SRB) 4-6 6-4 6-3 1-6 6-3

Nicolas Almagro (ESP) [26] beat Benjamin Becker (GER) 6-4 6-2 3-6 4-6
6-3

Alejandro Falla (COL) beat Marcel Granollers (ESP) 6-4 6-1 6-3

Andy Roddick (USA) [7] beat Thomaz Bellucci (BRA) 6-3 6-4 6-4

Feliciano Lopez (ESP) beat Rainer Schuettler (GER) 6-3 2-6 6-3 6-2

Evgeny Korolev (KAZ) beat Tomas Berdych (CZE) [21] 6-4 6-4 7-5

Fernando Gonzalez (CHI) [11] beat Marsel Ilhan (TUR) 6-3 6-4 7-5

Marin Cilic (CRO) [14] beat Bernard Tomic (AUS) 6-7 6-3 4-6 6-2 6-4

Stanislas Wawrinka (SUI) [19] beat Igor Kunitsyn (RUS) 6-3 6-2 6-2

Florian Mayer (GER) beat Viktor Troicki (SRB) [29] 4-6 6-4 7-6 6-1

Juan Martin Del Potro (ARG) [4] beat James Blake (USA) 6-4 6-7 5-7 6-3
10-8

Andy Murray (GBR) [5] beat Marc Gicquel (FRA) 6-1 6-4 6-3

Florent Serra (FRA) beat Jarkko Nieminen (FIN) 3-6 6-4 5-7 7-6 7-5

John Isner (USA) [33] beat Louk Sorensen (IRL) 6-3 7-6 7-5

Gael Monfils (FRA) [12] beat Antonio Veic (CRO) 6-4 6-4 6-4

Ivo Karlovic (CRO) beat Julien Benneteau (FRA) 2-6 6-1 6-3 6-3

Ivan Ljubicic (CRO) [24] beat Andrey Golubev (KAZ) 6-3 3-6 6-2 6-3

Philipp Kohlschreiber (GER) [27] beat Wayne Odesnik (USA) 6-4 3-6 6-3 6-2

Rafael Nadal (ESP) [2] beat Lukas Lacko (SVK) 6-2 6-2 6-2

Round 3

Roger Federer (SUI) [1] beat Albert Montanes (ESP) [31] 6-3 6-4 6-4

Lleyton Hewitt (AUS) [22] beat Marcos Baghdatis (CYP) 6-0 4-2 *(Baghdatis retired)*

Fernando Verdasco (ESP) [9] beat Stefan Koubek (AUT) 6-1 *(Koubek retired)*

Nikolay Davydenko (RUS) [6] beat Juan Monaco (ARG) [30] 6-0 6-3 6-4

Novak Djokovic (SRB) [3] beat Denis Istomin (UZB) 6-1 6-1 6-2

Lukasz Kubot (POL) beat Mikhail Youzhny (RUS) [20] *w/o*

Jo-Wilfried Tsonga (FRA) [10] beat Tommy Haas (GER) [18] 6-4 3-6 6-1 7-5

Nicolas Almagro (ESP) [26] beat Alejandro Falla (COL) 6-4 6-3 6-4

Andy Roddick (USA) [7] beat Feliciano Lopez (ESP) 6-7 6-4 6-4 7-6

Fernando Gonzalez (CHI) [11] beat Evgeny Korolev (KAZ) 6-7 6-3 6-1 6-3 6-4

Marin Cilic (CRO) [14] beat Stanislas Wawrinka (SUI) [19] 4-6 6-4 6-3 6-3

Juan Martin Del Potro (ARG) [4] beat Florian Mayer (GER) 6-3 0-6 6-4 7-5

Andy Murray (GBR) [5] beat Florent Serra (FRA) 7-5 6-1 6-4

John Isner (USA) [33] beat Gael Monfils (FRA) [12] 6-1 4-6 7-6 7-6

Ivo Karlovic (CRO) beat Ivan Ljubicic (CRO) [24] 6-3 3-6 7-6

Rafael Nadal (ESP) [2] beat Philipp Kohlschreiber (GER) [27] 6-4 6-2 2-6 7-5

Round 4

Roger Federer (SUI) [1] beat Lleyton Hewitt (AUS) [22] 6-2 6-3 6-4

Nikolay Davydenko (RUS) [6] beat Fernando Verdasco (ESP) [9] 6-2 7-5 4-6 6-7 6-3

Novak Djokovic (SRB) [3] beat Lukasz Kubot (POL) 6-1 6-2 7-5

Jo-Wilfried Tsonga (FRA) [10] beat Nicolas Almagro (ESP) [26] 6-3 6-4 4-6 6-7 9-7

Andy Roddick (USA) [7] beat Fernando Gonzalez (CHI) [11] 6-3 3-6 4-6 7-5 6-2

Marin Cilic (CRO) [14] beat Juan Martin Del Potro (ARG) [4] 5–7 6–4 7–5
5–7 6–3

Andy Murray (GBR) [5] beat John Isner (USA) [33] 7–6 6–3 6–2

Rafael Nadal (ESP) [2] beat Ivo Karlovic 6–4 4–6 6–4 6–4

Quarter-finals

Roger Federer (SUI) [1] beat Nikolay Davydenko (RUS) [6] 2–6 6–3 6–0 7–5

Jo-Wilfried Tsonga (FRA) [10] beat Novak Djokovic (SRB) [3] 7–6 6–7 1–6
6–3 6–1

Marin Cilic (CRO) [14] beat Andy Roddick (USA) [7] 7–6 6–3 3–6 2–6 6–3

Andy Murray (GBR) [5] beat Rafael Nadal (ESP) [2] 6–3 7–6 3–0
(Nadal retired)

Semi-finals

Roger Federer (SUI) [1] beat Jo-Wilfried Tsonga (FRA) [10] 6–2 6–3 6–2

**Andy Murray (GBR) [5] beat Marin Cilic (CRO) [14] 3–6 6–4 6–4
6–2**

Final

Roger Federer (SUI) [1] beat Andy Murray (GBR) [5] 6–3 6–4 7–6

Australian Open 2011

Round 1

Rafael Nadal (ESP) [1] beat Marcos Daniel (BRA) 6-0 5-0 *(Daniel retired)*

Ryan Sweeting (USA) beat Daniel Gimeno-Traver (ESP) 6-4 6-4 6-1

Bernard Tomic (AUS) beat Jeremy Chardy (FRA) 6-3 6-2 7-6

Feliciano Lopez (ESP) [31] beat Alejandro Falla (COL) 6-3 7-6 6-3

John Isner (USA) [20] beat Florent Serra (FRA) 6-3 7-6 6-3

Radek Stepanek (CZE) beat Denis Gremelmayr (GER) 6-3 6-2 6-3

Santiago Giraldo (COL) beat Rui Machado (POR) 6-4 6-3 5-7 6-1

Marin Cilic (CRO) [15] beat Donald Young (USA) 6-3 6-2 6-1

Mikhail Youzhny (RUS) [10] beat Marsel Ilhan (TUR) 6-2 6-3 7-6

Blaz Kavcic (SLO) beat Kevin Anderson (RSA) 2-6 6-4 7-6 7-6

Milos Raonic (CAN) beat Bjorn Phau (GER) 7-6 6-3 7-6

Michael Llodra (FRA) [22] beat Juan Ignacio Chela (ARG) 6-3 3-6 6-2 6-4

David Nalbandian (ARG) [27] beat Lleyton Hewitt (AUS) 3-6 6-4 3-6 7-6 9-7

Richard Berankis (LTU) beat Marinko Matosevic (AUS) 6-4 6-2 7-5

Michael Russell (USA) beat Matthew Ebden (AUS) 6-3 6-2 5-7 7-6

David Ferrer (ESP) [7] beat Jarkko Nieminen (FIN) 6-4 6-3 1-6 6-2

Robin Soderling (SWE) [4] beat Potito Starace (ITA) 6-4 6-2 6-2

Gilles Muller (LUX) beat Simon Stadler (GER) 6-3 7-6 6-4

Jan Hernych (CZE) beat Denis Istomin (UZB) 6-3 6-4 3-6 6-2

Thomaz Bellucci (BRA) [30] beat Ricardo Mello (BRA) 7-5 7-5 4-6 3-6 6-3

Benjamin Becker (GER) beat Ernests Gulbis (LAT) [24] 7-6 6-2 6-4

Alexandr Dolgopolov (UKR) beat Mikhail Kukushkin (KAZ) 6-3 6-2 6-4

Andreas Seppi (ITA) beat Arnaud Clement (FRA) 3-6 2-6 7-5 6-3 6-2

Jo-Wilfried Tsonga (FRA) [13] beat Philipp Petzschner (GER) 4-6 2-6 6-2 6-3 6-4

Jurgen Melzer (AUT) [11] beat Vincent Millot (FRA) 6-2 6-4 6-2

Pere Riba (ESP) beat Carsten Ball (AUS) 6-1 6-7 2-6 6-2 4-6

Juan Martin Del Potro (ARG) beat Dudi Sela (ISR) 7-6 6-4 6-4

Marcos Baghdatis (CYP) [21] beat Grega Zemlja (SLO) 3-6 7-5 6-1 4-6 6-2

Guillermo Garcia-Lopez (ESP) [32] beat Michael Berrer (GER) 6-4 6-4 3-6 6-3

Eduardo Schwank (ARG) beat Leonardo Mayer (ARG) 6-2 6-0 6-4

Illya Marchenko (UKR) beat Ruben Ramirez Hidalgo (ESP) 6-3 6-4 6-1

Andy Murray (GBR) [5] beat Karol Beck (SVK) 6-3 6-1 4-2 (Beck retired)

Tomas Berdych (CZE) [6] beat Marco Crugnola (ITA) 6-4 6-0 6-2

Philipp Kohlschreiber (GER) beat Tobias Kamke (GER) 1-6 4-6 7-6 6-4 6-4

Adrian Mannarino (FRA) beat Ryan Harrison (USA) 6-4 6-3 6-4

Richard Gasquet (FRA) [28] beat Frank Dancevic (CAN) 6-3 6-4 6-4

Florian Mayer (GER) beat Nikolay Davydenko (RUS) [23] 6-3 4-6 7-6 6-4

Kei Nishikori (JPN) beat Fabio Fognini (ITA) 6-1 6-4 6-7 6-4

Janko Tipsarevic (SRB) beat Mischa Zverev (GER) 6-3 6-1 6-4

Fernando Verdasco (ESP) [9] beat Rainer Schuettler (GER) 6-1 6-3 6-2

Nicolas Almagro (ESP) [14] beat Stephane Robert (FRA) 6-4 6-3 6-7 7-5

Igor Andreev (RUS) beat Filippo Volandri (ITA) 6-3 7-6 6-3
Benoit Paire (FRA) beat Flavio Cipolla (ITA) 6-1 7-5 6-1
Ivan Ljubicic (CRO) [17] beat Peter Luczak (AUS) 6-3 6-3 7-6
Viktor Troicki (SRB) [29] beat Dmitry Tursunov (RUS) 6-2 3-6 6-2 6-0
Nicolas Mahut (FRA) beat Brian Dabul (ARG) 6-3 6-4 6-4
Ivan Dodig (CRO) beat Ivo Karlovic (CRO) 6-4 3-6 6-7 6-4 6-4
Novak Djokovic (SRB) [3] beat Marcel Granollers (ESP) 6-1 6-3 6-1

Andy Roddick (USA) [8] beat Jan Hajek (CZE) 6-1 6-2 6-2
Igor Kunitsyn (RUS) beat Michal Przysiezny (POL) 6-7 6-4 6-4 7-6
Robin Haase (NED) beat Carlos Berlocq (ARG) 6-4 6-3 7-6
Juan Monaco (ARG) [26] beat Simon Greul (GER) 7-6 7-6 6-2
Stanislas Wawrinka (SUI) [19] beat Teymuraz Gabashvili (RUS) 7-6 6-4 6-4
Grigor Dimitrov (BUL) beat Andrey Golubev (KAZ) 6-1 6-4 6-2
Frederico Gil (POR) beat Pablo Cuevas (URU) 6-4 6-7 4-6 6-3 9-7
Gael Monfils (FRA) [12] beat Thiemo de Bakker (NED) 6-7 2-6 7-5 6-2
    6-1
Mardy Fish (USA) [16] beat Victor Hanescu (ROU) 2-6 4-6 6-3 7-5 6-3
Tommy Robredo (ESP) beat Somdev Devvarman (IND) 7-6 6-3 6-4
Sergiy Stakhovsky (UKR) beat Daniel Brands (GER) 6-2 6-3 6-4
Lukasz Kubot (POL) beat Sam Querrey (USA) [18] 5-7 6-2 3-6 6-1 8-6
Albert Montanes (ESP) [25] beat Dustin Brown (GER) 6-4 6-2 3-6 2-6 7-5
Xavier Malisse (BEL) beat Pablo Andujar (ESP) 6-1 6-2 7-6
Gilles Simon (FRA) beat Yen-Hsun Lu (TPE) 6-7 6-2 6-4 6-2
Roger Federer (SUI) [2] (TPE) beat Lukas Lacko (SVK) 6-1 6-1 6-3

Round 2

Rafael Nadal (ESP) [1] beat Ryan Sweeting (USA) 6-2 6-1 6-1
Bernard Tomic (AUS) beat Feliciano Lopez (ESP) [31] 7-6 7-6 6-3
John Isner (USA) [20] beat Radek Stepanek (CZE) 4-6 6-4 6-2 6-1
Marin Cilic (CRO) [15] beat Santiago Giraldo (COL) 6-3 7-6 6-1
Mikhail Youzhny (RUS) [10] beat Blaz Kavcic (SLO) 6-3 6-1 5-7 4-6 6-1

Milos Raonic (CAN) beat Michael Llodra (FRA) [22] 7-6 6-3 7-6

Richard Berankis (LTU) beat David Nalbandian (ARG) [27] 6-1 6-0 2-0
 (Nalbandian retired)

David Ferrer (ESP) [7] beat David Ferrer (ESP) [7] 6-0 6-1 7-5

Robin Soderling (SWE) [4] beat Gilles Muller (LUX) 6-3 7-6 6-1

Jan Hernych (CZE) beat Thomaz Bellucci (BRA) [30] 6-2 6-7 6-4 6-7 8-6

Alexandr Dolgopolov (UKR) beat Benjamin Becker (GER) 6-3 6-0 3-6 7-6

Jo-Wilfried Tsonga (FRA) [13] beat Andreas Seppi (ITA) 6-3 7-6 7-6

Jurgen Melzer (AUT) [11] beat Pere Riba (ESP) 6-2 6-4 6-2

Marcos Baghdatis (CYP) [21] beat Juan Martin Del Potro (ARG) 6-1 6-3
 4-6 6-3

Guillermo Garcia-Lopez (ESP) [32] beat Eduardo Schwank (ARG) 6-4 7-6
 6-1

Andy Murray (GBR) [5] beat Illya Marchenko (UKR) 6-1 6-3 6-3

Tomas Berdych (CZE) [6] beat Philipp Kohlschreiber (GER) 4-6 6-2 6-3 6-4

Richard Gasquet (FRA) [28] beat Adrian Mannarino (FRA) 6-3 7-6 6-4

Kei Nishikori (JPN) beat Florian Mayer (GER) 6-4 6-3 0-6 6-3

Fernando Verdasco (ESP) [9] beat Janko Tipsarevic (SRB) 2-6 4-6 6-4 7-6
 6-0

Nicolas Almagro (ESP) [14] beat Igor Andreev (RUS) 7-5 2-6 4-6 7-6 7-5

Ivan Ljubicic (CRO) [17] beat Benoit Paire (FRA) 6-3 6-7 6-4 7-6

Viktor Troicki (SRB) [29] beat Nicolas Mahut (FRA) 6-4 6-2 1-6 6-3

Novak Djokovic (SRB) [3] beat Ivan Dodig (CRO) 7-5 6-7 6-0 6-2

Andy Roddick (USA) [8] beat Igor Kunitsyn (RUS) 7-6 6-2 6-3

Robin Haase (NED) beat Juan Monaco (ARG) [26] 6-4 6-4 3-6 6-2

Stanislas Wawrinka (SUI) [19] beat Grigor Dimitrov (BUL) 7-5 6-3 6-3

Gael Monfils (FRA) [12] beat Frederico Gil (POR) 6-4 6-3 1-6 6-2

Tommy Robredo (ESP) beat Mardy Fish (USA) [16] 1-6 6-3 6-3 6-3

Sergiy Stakhovsky (UKR) beat Lukasz Kubot (POL) 6-3 6-4 6-4

Xavier Malisse (BEL) beat Albert Montanes (ESP) [25] 6-4 6-0 6-1

Roger Federer (SUI) [2] beat Gilles Simon (FRA) 6-2 6-3 4-6 4-6 6-3

Round 3

Rafael Nadal (ESP) [1] beat Bernard Tomic (AUS) 6-2 7-5 6-3

Marin Cilic (CRO) [15] beat John Isner (USA) [20] 4-6 6-2 6-7 7-6 9-7

Milos Raonic (CAN) beat Mikhail Youzhny (RUS) [10] 6-4 7-5 4-6 6-4

David Ferrer (ESP) [7] beat Richard Berankis (LTU) 6-2 6-2 6-1

Robin Soderling (SWE) [4] beat Jan Hernych (CZE) 6-3 6-1 6-4

Alexandr Dolgopolov (UKR) beat Jo-Wilfried Tsonga (FRA) [13] 3-6 6-3
3-6 6-1 6-1

Jurgen Melzer (AUT) [11] beat Marcos Baghdatis (CYP) [21] 6-7 6-2 6-1
4-3 *(Baghdatis retired)*

**Andy Murray (GBR) [5] beat Guillermo Garcia-Lopez (ESP) [32]
6-1 6-1 6-2**

Tomas Berdych (CZE) [6] beat Richard Gasquet (FRA) [28] 6-2 7-6 6-2

Fernando Verdasco (ESP) [9] beat Kei Nishikori (JPN) 6-2 6-4 6-3

Nicolas Almagro (ESP) [14] beat Ivan Ljubicic (CRO) [17] 6-4 7-6 6-3

Novak Djokovic (SRB) [3] beat Viktor Troicki (SRB) [29] 6-2 *(Troicki retired)*

Andy Roddick (USA) [8] beat Robin Haase (NED) 2-6 7-6 6-2 6-2

Stanislas Wawrinka (SUI) [19] beat Gael Monfils (FRA) [12] 7-6 6-2 6-3

Tommy Robredo (ESP) beat Sergiy Stakhovsky (UKR) 5-7 6-2 6-4 6-2

Roger Federer (SUI) [2] beat Xavier Malisse (BEL) 6-3 6-3 6-1

Round 4

Rafael Nadal (ESP) [1] beat Marin Cilic (CRO) [15] 6-2 6-4 6-3

David Ferrer (ESP) [7] beat Milos Raonic (CAN) 4-6 6-2 6-3 6-4

Alexandr Dolgopolov (UKR) beat Robin Soderling (SWE) [4] 1-6 6-3 6-1
4-6 6-2

Andy Murray (GBR) [5] beat Jurgen Melzer (AUT) [11] 6-3 6-1 6-1

Tomas Berdych (CZE) [6] beat Fernando Verdasco (ESP) [9] 6-4 6-2 6-3

Novak Djokovic (SRB) [3] beat Nicolas Almagro (ESP) [14] 6-3 6-4 6-0

Stanislas Wawrinka (SUI) [19] beat Andy Roddick (USA) [8] 6-3 6-4 6-4

Roger Federer (SUI) [2] beat Tommy Robredo (ESP) 6-3 3-6 6-3 6-2

Quarter-finals

David Ferrer (ESP) [7] beat Rafael Nadal (ESP) [1] 6-4 6-2 6-3

Andy Murray (GBR) [5] beat Alexandr Dolgopolov (UKR) 7-5 6-3 6-7 6-3

Novak Djokovic (SRB) [3] beat Tomas Berdych (CZE) [6] 6-1 7-6 6-1

Roger Federer (SUI) [2] beat Stanislas Wawrinka (SUI) [19] 6-1 6-3 6-3

Semi-finals

Andy Murray (GBR) [5] beat David Ferrer (ESP) [7] 4-6 7-6 6-1 7-6

Novak Djokovic (SRB) [3] beat Roger Federer (SUI) [2] 7-6 7-5 6-4

Final

Novak Djokovic (SRB) [3] beat Andy Murray (GBR [5] 6-4 6-2 6-3

Australian Open 2013
Round 1

Novak Djokovic (SRB) [1] beat Paul-Henri Mathieu (FRA) 6-2 6-4 7-5

Ryan Harrison (USA) beat Santiago Giraldo (COL) 2-6 6-4 7-5 6-4

Feliciano Lopez (ESP) beat Arnau Brugues-Davi (ESP) 6-3 6-2 6-4

Radek Stepanek (CZE) [31] beat Viktor Troicki (SRB) 5-7 4-6 6-3 6-3 7-5

Sam Querrey (USA) [20] beat Daniel Munoz-De La Nava (ESP) 6-7 6-4 6-2
6-4

Brian Baker (USA) beat Alex Bogomolov Jr. (RUS) 7-6 6-3 6-7 3-6 6-2

Tobias Kamke (GER) beat Flavio Cipolla (ITA) 6-1 6-4 6-1

Stanislas Wawrinka (SUI) [15] beat Cedrik-Marcel Stebe (GER) 6-2 6-4 6-3

Andrey Kuznetsov (RUS) beat Juan Monaco (ARG) [11] 7-6 6-1 6-1

Kevin Anderson (RSA) beat Paolo Lorenzi (ITA) 3-6 7-6 6-3 6-4

Xavier Malisse (BEL) beat Pablo Andujar (ESP) 6-3 6-1 6-2

Fernando Verdasco (ESP) [22] beat David Goffin (BEL) 6-3 3-6 4-6 6-3 6-4

Jurgen Melzer (AUT) [26] beat Mikhail Kukushkin (KAZ) 6-1 6-1 6-2

Roberto Bautista Agut (ESP) beat Fabio Fognini (ITA) 6-0 2-6 6-4 3-6 6-1

Guillaume Rufin (FRA) beat Julian Reister (GER) 4-6 7-6 6-1 6-2
Tomas Berdych (CZE) [5] beat Michael Russell (USA) 6-3 7-5 6-3

David Ferrer (ESP) [4] beat Olivier Rochus (BEL) 6-3 6-4 6-2
Tim Smyczek (USA) beat Ivo Karlovic (CRO) 6-4 7-6 7-5
Tatsuma Ito (JPN) beat John Millman (AUS) 6-4 6-4 3-6 0-6 7-5
Marcos Baghdatis (CYP) [28] beat Albert Ramos (ESP) 6-7 7-6 6-4 3-6 6-3
Mikhail Youzhny (RUS) [23] beat Matthew Ebden (AUS) 4-6 6-7 6-2 7-6
    6-3
Evgeny Donskoy (RUS) beat Adrian Ungur (ROU) 6-4 6-4 6-2
Carlos Berlocq (ARG) beat Maxime Authom (BEL) 1-6 7-6 7-6 6-2
Kei Nishikori (JPN) [16] beat Victor Hanescu (ROU) 6-7 6-3 6-1 6-3
Nicolas Almagro (ESP) [10] beat Steve Johnson (USA) 7-5 6-7 6-2 6-7 6-2
Daniel Gimeno-Traver (ESP) beat Lukasz Kubot (POL) 6-7 6-4 6-0 4-6 6-4
Somdev Devvarman (IND) beat Bjorn Phau (GER) 6-3 6-2 6-3
Jerzy Janowicz (POL) [24] beat Simone Bolelli (ITA) 7-5 6-4 6-3
Julien Benneteau (FRA) [32] beat Grigor Dimitrov (BUL) 6-4 6-2 6-4
Edouard Roger-Vasselin (FRA) beat Ruben Bemelmans (BEL) 6-3 6-7 2-6
    7-5 11-9
Lukas Lacko (SVK) beat Gilles Muller (LUX) 6-2 6-4 7-6
Janko Tipsarevic (SRB) [8] beat Lleyton Hewitt (AUS) 7-6 7-5 6-3

Juan Martin Del Potro (ARG) [6] beat Adrian Mannarino (FRA) 6-1 6-2
    6-2
Benjamin Becker (GER) beat Aljaz Bedene (SLO) 4-6 6-3 7-5 7-6
Jeremy Chardy (FRA) beat Adrian Menendez-Maceiras (ESP) 7-6 6-7 6-2
    6-1
Marcel Granollers (ESP) [30] beat Grega Zemlja (SLO) 7-6 7-6 1-0 *(Zemlja
    retired)*
Andreas Seppi (ITA) [21] beat Horacio Zeballos (ARG) 6-2 6-4 6-2
Denis Istomin (UZB) beat Igor Sijsling (NED) 4-6 6-3 6-4 6-2
Rajeev Ram (USA) beat Guillermo Garcia-Lopez (ESP) 6-4 6-4 3-6 6-2
Marin Cilic (CRO) [12] beat Marinko Matosevic (AUS) 6-4 7-5 6-2

Gilles Simon (FRA) [14] beat Filippo Volandri (ITA) 2-6 6-3 6-2 6-2
Jesse Levine (CAN) beat Tommy Robredo (ESP) 7-6 6-7 6-4 6-4
Ruben Ramirez Hidalgo (ESP) beat Yen-Hsun Lu (TPE) 6-2 6-1 4-6 6-1
Gael Monfils (FRA) beat Alexandr Dolgopolov (UKR) [18] 6-7 7-6 6-3 6-3
Florian Mayer (GER) [25] beat Rhyne Williams (USA) 2-6 3-6 6-2 7-6 6-1
Ricardas Berankis (LTU) beat Sergiy Stakhovsky (UKR) 6-2 7-6 7-5
Joao Sousa (POR) beat John-Patrick Smith (AUS) 6-4 6-1 6-4
Andy Murray (GBR) [3] beat Robin Haase (NED) 6-3 6- 6-3

Jo-Wilfried Tsonga (FRA) [7] beat Michael Llodra (FRA) 6-4 7-5 6-2
Go Soeda (JPN) beat Luke Saville (AUS) 6-7 6-3 6-2 6-3
James Duckworth (AUS) beat Benjamin Mitchell (AUS) 6-4 7-6 4-6 5-7 8-6
Blaz Kavcic (SLO) beat Thomaz Bellucci (BRA) [29] 6-3 6-1 6-3
Jarkko Nieminen (FIN) beat Tommy Haas (GER) [19] 7-6 4-6 6-3 4-6 8-6
Ivan Dodig (CRO) beat Di Wu (CHN) 7-5 4-6 6-3 6-3
Alejandro Falla (COL) beat Josselin Ouanna (FRA) 6-4 7-5 6-4
Richard Gasquet (FRA) [9] beat Albert Montanes (ESP) 7-5 6-2 6-1
Milos Raonic (CAN) [13] beat Jan Hajek (CZE) 3-6 6-1 6-2 7-6
Lukas Rosol (CZE) beat Jamie Baker (GBR) 7-6 7-5 6-2
Amir Weintraub (ISR) beat Guido Pella (ARG) 7-6 7-5 6-2
Philipp Kohlschreiber (GER) [17] beat Steve Darcis (BEL) 6-2 6-3 6-4
Daniel Brands (GER) beat Martin Klizan (SVK) [27] 6-3 3-6 6-3 6-4
Bernard Tomic (AUS) beat Leonardo Mayer (ARG) 6-3 6-2 6-3
Nikolay Davydenko (RUS) beat Dudi Sela (ISR) 3-6 6-1 7-5 6-3
Roger Federer (SUI) [2] beat Benoit Paire (FRA) 6-2 6-4 6-1

Round 2

Novak Djokovic (SRB) [1] beat Ryan Harrison (USA) 6-1 6-2 6-3
Radek Stepanek (CZE) [31] beat Feliciano Lopez (ESP) 6-2 6-2 6-4
Sam Querrey (USA) [20] beat Brian Baker (USA) 6-7 1-1 *(Baker retired)*
Stanislas Wawrinka (SUI) [15] beat Tobias Kamke (GER) 6-3 7-6 *(Kamke retired)*

Kevin Anderson (RSA) beat Andrey Kuznetsov (RUS) 6-1 7-5 6-4

Fernando Verdasco (ESP) [22] beat Xavier Malisse (BEL) 6-1 6-3 6-2

Jurgen Melzer (AUT) [26] beat Roberto Bautista Agut (ESP) 6-7 6-3 6-7 6-3
6-2

Tomas Berdych (CZE) [5] beat Guillaume Rufin (FRA) 6-2 6-2 6-4

David Ferrer (ESP) [4] beat Tim Smyczek (USA) 6-0 7-5 4-6 6-3

Marcos Baghdatis (CYP) [28] beat Tatsuma Ito (JPN) 3-6 6-3 6-2 6-2

Evgeny Donskoy (RUS) beat Mikhail Youzhny (RUS) [23] 3-6 6-7 6-2 3-6
6-3

Kei Nishikori (JPN) [16] beat Carlos Berlocq (ARG) 7-6 6-4 6-1

Nicolas Almagro (ESP) [10] beat Daniel Gimeno-Traver (ESP) 6-4 6-1 6-2

Jerzy Janowicz (POL) [24] beat Somdev Devvarman (IND) 6-7 3-6 6-1 6-0
7-5

Julien Benneteau (FRA) [32] beat Edouard Roger-Vasselin (FRA) 4-6 7-5
7-6 7-6

Janko Tipsarevic (SRB) [8] beat Lukas Lacko (SVK) 6-3 6-4 3-6 4-6 7-5

Juan Martin Del Potro (ARG) [6] beat Benjamin Becker (GER) 6-2 6-4 6-2

Jeremy Chardy (FRA) beat Marcel Granollers (ESP) [30] 6-3 3-6 6-1 6-2

Andreas Seppi (ITA) [21] beat Denis Istomin (UZB) 7-6 5-7 6-7 7-6 6-2

Marin Cilic (CRO) [12] beat Rajeev Ram (USA) 7-5 6-2 6-4

Gilles Simon (FRA) [14] beat Jesse Levine (CAN) 2-6 6-3 7-6 6-2

Gael Monfils (FRA) beat Yen-Hsun Lu (TPE) 7-6 4-6 0-6 6-1 8-6

Ricardas Berankis (LTU) beat Florian Mayer (GER) [25] 6-2 6-3 6-1

Andy Murray (GBR) [3] beat Joao Sousa (POR) 6-2 6-2 6-4

Jo-Wilfried Tsonga (FRA) [7] beat Go Soeda (JPN) 6-3 7-6 6-3

Blaz Kavcic (SLO) beat James Duckworth (AUS) 3-6 6-3 6-4 6-7 10-8

Ivan Dodig (CRO) beat Jarkko Nieminen (FIN) 6-3 6-7 6-3 6-7 6-1

Richard Gasquet (FRA) [9] beat Alejandro Falla (COL) 6-3 6-2 6-2

Milos Raonic (CAN) [13] beat Lukas Rosol (CZE) 7-6 6-2 6-3

Philipp Kohlschreiber (GER) [17] beat Amir Weintraub (ISR) 6-2 7-6 6-4

Bernard Tomic (AUS) beat Daniel Brands (GER) 6-7 7-5 7-6 7-6

Roger Federer (SUI) [2] beat Nikolay Davydenko (RUS) 6-3 6-4 6-4

Round 3

Novak Djokovic (SRB) [1] beat Radek Stepanek (CZE) [31] 6-4 6-3 7-5
Stanislas Wawrinka (SUI) [15] beat Sam Querrey (USA) [20] 7-6 7-5 6-4
Kevin Anderson (RSA) beat Fernando Verdasco (ESP) [22] 4-6 6-3 4-6 7-6
  6-2
Tomas Berdych (CZE) [5] beat Jurgen Melzer (AUT) [26] 6-3 6-2 6-2
David Ferrer (ESP) [4] beat Marcos Baghdatis (CYP) [28] 6-4 6-2 6-3
Kei Nishikori (JPN) [16] beat Evgeny Donskoy (RUS) 7-6 6-2 6-3
Nicolas Almagro (ESP) [10] beat Jerzy Janowicz (POL) [24] 7-6 7-6 6-1
Janko Tipsarevic (SRB) [8] beat Julien Benneteau (FRA) [32] 3-6 6-4 2-6
  6-4 6-3
Jeremy Chardy (FRA) beat Juan Martin Del Potro (ARG) [6] 6-3 6-3 6-7
  3-6 6-3
Andreas Seppi (ITA) [21] beat Marin Cilic (CRO) [12] 6-7 6-3 2-6 6-4 6-2
Gilles Simon (FRA) [14] beat Gael Monfils (FRA) 6-4 6-4 4-6 1-6 8-6
Andy Murray (GBR) [3] beat Ricardas Berankis (LTU) 6-3 6-4 7-5
Jo-Wilfried Tsonga (FRA) [7] beat Blaz Kavcic (SLO) 6-2 6-1 6-4
Ivan Dodig (CRO) beat Richard Gasquet (FRA) [9] 4-6 6-3 7-6 6-0
Milos Raonic (CAN) [13] beat Philipp Kohlschreiber (GER) [17] 7-6 6-3
  6-4
Roger Federer (SUI) [2] beat Bernard Tomic (AUS) 6-4 7-6 6-1

Round 4

Novak Djokovic (SRB) [1] beat Stanislas Wawrinka (SUI) [15] 1-6 7-5 6-4
  6-7 12-10
Tomas Berdych (CZE) [5] beat Kevin Anderson (RSA) 6-3 6-2 7-6
David Ferrer (ESP) [4] beat Kei Nishikori (JPN) [16] 6-2 6-1 6-4
Nicolas Almagro (ESP) [10] beat Janko Tipsarevic (SRB) [8] 6-2 5-1
  (Tipsarevic retired)
Jeremy Chardy (FRA) beat Andreas Seppi (ITA) [21] 5-7 6-3 6-2 6-2
Andy Murray (GBR) [3] beat Gilles Simon (FRA) [14] 6-3 6-1 6-3

Jo-Wilfried Tsonga (FRA) [7] beat Richard Gasquet (FRA) [9] 6-4 3-6 6-3
6-2

Roger Federer (SUI) [2] beat Milos Raonic (CAN) [13] 6-4 7-6 6-2

Quarter-finals

Novak Djokovic (SRB) [1] beat Tomas Berdych (CZE) [5] 6-1 4-6 6-1 6-4

David Ferrer (ESP) [4] beat Nicolas Almagro (ESP) [10] 4-6 4-6 7-5 7-6 6-2

Andy Murray (GBR) [3] beat Jeremy Chardy (FRA) 6-4 6-1 6-2

Roger Federer (SUI) [2] beat Jo-Wilfried Tsonga (FRA) [7] 7-6 4-6 7-6 3-6
6-3

Semi-finals

Novak Djokovic (SRB) [1] beat David Ferrer (ESP) [4] 6-2 6-2 6-1

**Andy Murray (GBR) [3] beat Roger Federer (SUI) [2] 6-4 6-7 6-3
6-7 6-2**

Final

**Novak Djokovic (SRB) [1] beat Andy Murray (GBR) [3] 6-7 7-6 6-3
6-2**

Olympics 2012
Men's Singles
Round 1

Roger Federer (SUI) [1] beat Alejandro Falla (COL) 6-3 5-7 6-3

Julien Benneteau (FRA) beat Mikhail Youzhny (RUS) 7-5 6-3

Gilles Müller (LUX) beat Adrian Ungur (ROU) 6-3 6-3

Denis Istomin (UZB) beat Fernando Verdasco (ESP) [14] 6-4 7-6

John Isner (USA) [10] beat Olivier Rochus (BEL) 7-6 6-4

Malek Jaziri (TUN) beat Yen-hsun Lu (TPE) 7-6 4-6 6-3

Philipp Petzschner (GER) beat Lukas Lacko (SVK) 7-6 6-1

Janko Tipsarević (SRB) [7] beat David Nalbandian (ARG) 6-3 6-4

David Ferrer (ESP) [4] beat Vasek Pospisil (CAN) 6-4 6-4

Blaz Kavčič (SLO) beat Vishnu Vardhan (IND) 6-3 6-2

Nikolay Davydenko (RUS) beat Radek Štěpánek (CZE) 6-4 6-3

Kei Nishikori (JPN) [15] beat Bernard Tomic (AUS) 6-4 6-4

Gilles Simon (FRA) [12] beat Mikhail Kukushkin (KAZ) 6-4 6-2

Grigor Dimitrov (BUL) beat Lukasz Kubot (POL) 6-3 7-6

Andreas Seppi (ITA) beat Donald Young (USA) 6-4 6-4
Juan Martin del Potro (ARG) [8] beat I Dodig (CRO) 6-4 6-1

Steve Darcis (BEL) beat Tomas Berdych (CZE) [6] 6-4 6-4
Santiago Giraldo (COL) beat Ryan Harrison (USA) 7-5 6-3
Alex Bogomolov, Jr. (RUS) beat Carlos Berlocq (ARG) 7-5 7-6
Nicolas Almagro (ESP) [11] beat Viktor Troicki (SRB) 6-4 7-6
Richard Gasquet (FRA) [16] beat Robin Haase (NED) 6-3 6-3
Marcos Baghdatis (CYP) beat Go Soeda (JPN) 6-7 7-6 6-2
Jarkko Nieminen (FIN) beat Somdev Devvarman (IND) 6-3 6-1
Andy Murray (GBR) [3] beat Stanislav Wawrinka (SUI) 6-3 6-3
Jo-Wilfried Tsonga (FRA) [5] beat Thomaz Bellucci (BRA) 6-7 6-4 6-4
Milos Raonic (CAN) beat Tatsuma Ito (JPN) 6-3 6-4
Feliciano López (ESP) beat Dmitry Tursunov (RUS) 6-7 6-2 9-7
Juan Mónaco (ARG) [9] beat David Goffin (BEL) 6-4 6-1
Marin Čilić (CRO) [13] beat Jürgen Melzer (AUT) 7-6 6-2
Lleyton Hewitt (AUS) beat Sergiy Stakhovsky (UKR) 6-3 4-6 6-3
Andy Roddick (USA) beat Martin Kližan (SVK) 7-5 6-4
Novak Djokovic (SRB) [2] beat Fabio Fognini (ITA)

Round 2

Roger Federer (SUI) [1] beat Julien Benneteau 6-2 6-2
Denis Istomin (UZB) beat Gilles Müller (LUX) 6-7 7-6 7-5
John Isner (USA) [10] beat Malek Jaziri (TUN) 7-6 6-2
Janko Tipsarević (SRB) [7] beat Philipp Petzschner (GER) 3-6 6-3 6-4
David Ferrer (ESP) [4] beat Blaz Kavčič (SLO) 6-2 6-2
Kei Nishikori (JPN) [15] beat Nikolay Davydenko (RUS) 4-6 6-4 6-1
Gilles Simon (FRA) [12] beat Grigor Dimitrov (BUL) 6-3 6-3
Juan Martin del Potro (ARG) beat Andreas Seppi (ITA) 6-1 4-6 6-3
Steve Darcis (BEL) beat Santiago Giraldo (COL) 6-7 6-4 6-4
Nicolas Almagro (ESP) [11] beat Alex Bogomolov, Jr. (RUS) 6-2 6-2
Richard Gasquet (FRA) [16] beat Marcos Baghdatis (CYP) 6-4 6-4

Andy Murray (GBR) [3] beat Jarkko Nieminen (FIN) 6-2 6-4
Jo-Wilfried Tsonga (FRA) [5] beat Milos Raonic (CAN) 6-3 3-6 25-23
Feliciano López (ESP) beat Juan Mónaco (ARG) [9] 6-4 6-4
Lleyton Hewitt (AUS) beat Marin Čilić (CRO) [13] 6-4 7-5
Novak Djokovic (SRB) [2] beat Andy Roddick (USA) 6-2 6-1

Round 3

Roger Federer (SUI) [1] beat Denis Istomin (UZB) 7-5 6-3
John Isner (USA) [10] beat Janko Tipsarević (SRB) 7-5 7-6
Kei Nishikori (JPN) [15] beat David Ferrer (ESP) [4] 6-0 3-6 6-4
Juan Martin del Potro (ARG) beat Gilles Simon (FRA) [12] 6-1 4-6 6-3
Nicolas Almagro (ESP) [11] beat Steve Darcis (BEL) 7-5 6-3
**Andy Murray (GBR) [3] beat Richard Gasquet (FRA) [16] 4-6 6-1
6-4**
Jo-Wilfried Tsonga (FRA) [5] beat Feliciano López (ESP) 7-6 6-4
Novak Djokovic (SRB) [2] beat Lleyton Hewitt (AUS) 4-6 7-5 6-1

Quarter-finals

Roger Federer (SUI) [1] beat John Isner (USA) [10] 6-4 7-6
Juan Martin del Potro (ARG) beat Kei Nishikori (JPN) [15] 6-4 7-6
Andy Murray (GBR) [3] beat Nicolas Almagro (ESP) [11] 6-4 6-1
Novak Djokovic (SRB) [2] beat Jo-Wilfried Tsonga (FRA) [5] 6-1 7-5

Semi-finals

Roger Federer (SUI) [1] beat Juan Martin del Potro (ARG) 3-6 7-5 19-17
Andy Murray (GBR) [3] beat Novak Djokovic (SRB) [2] 7-5 7-5

Final

Andy Murray (GBR) [3] beat Roger Federer (SUI) [1] 6-2 6-1 6-4

Bronze medal match

Juan Martin del Potro (ARG) beat Novak Djokovic (SRB) [2] 7-5 6-4

Mixed Doubles

Note: If the set score was tied at one set all, a 'super tie-break' (the first pairing to win at least 10 points by a margin of two points) was played

Round 1

Victoria Azarenka & Max Mirnyi (BLR) [1] beat A Kerber & Philipp (GER) 6-2 6-2

Sania Mirza & Leandro Paes (IND] beat Ana Ivanovic & Nenad Zimonjić (SRB) 6-2 6-4

Lisa Raymond & Mike Bryan (USA) [3] beat Sara Erani & Andreas Seppi (ITA) 7-5 6-3

Gisela Dulko & Juan Martin Del Potro (ARG) beat Elena Vesnina & Mikhail Youzhny (RUS) 6-3 7-5

Laura Robson & Andy Murray (GBR) beat Lucie Hradecka & Radek Stepanek 7-5 6-7 [10-7]

Sam Stosur & Lleyton Hewitt (AUS) beat Agnieska Radwanska & Marcin Matkowski (POL) [4] 6-3 6-3

Roberta Vinci & Danieli Bracciali (ITA) beat Sofia Arvidsson & Robert Lindstedt (SWE) 6-3 4-6 [10-8]

Sabine Lisicki & Christopher Kas (GER) beat Liezel Huber & Bob Bryan (USA) [2] 7-6 6-7 [10-5]

Quarter-finals

Victoria Azarenka & Max Mirnyi (BLR) [1] beat Sania Mirza & Leandro Paes (IND] 7-5 7-6

Lisa Raymond & Mike Bryan (USA) [3] beat Gisela Dulko & Juan Martin
Del Potro (ARG) 6-2 7-5

**Laura Robson & Andy Murray (GBR) beat Sam Stosur & Lleyton
Hewitt (AUS) 6-3 3-6 [10-8]**

Sabine Lisicki & Christopher Kas (GER) beat Roberta Vinci & Danieli
Bracciali (ITA) 4-6 7-6 [10-7]

Semi-finals

Victoria Azarenka & Max Mirnyi (BLR) [1] beat Lisa Raymond & Mike
Bryan (USA) [3] 3-6 6-4 [10-7]

**Laura Robson & Andy Murray (GBR) beat Sabine Lisicki &
Christopher Kas (GER) 6-1 6-7 [10-7]**

Final

**Victoria Azarenka & Max Mirnyi (BLR) [1] beat Laura Robson &
Andy Murray (GBR) 2-6 6-3 [10-8]**

US Open 2008

Round 1

Rafa Nadal (ESP) [1] beat Björn Phau (GER) 7-6 6-3 7-6

Ryler DeHeart (USA) beat Olivier Rochus (BEL) 7-6 5-7 6-4 3-6 6-4

Viktor Troicki (SRB) beat Carsten Ball (AUS) 7-6 6-0 6-1

Philipp Kohlschreiber (GER) [25] beat Luis Horna (PER) 6-2 6-3 6-2

Sam Querrey (USA) beat Tomas Berdych (CZE) [22] 6-3 6-1 6-2

Nicolas Devilder (FRA) beat Pablo Anduljar (ESP) 6-4 6-2 6-2

Florent Serra (FRA) beat Rainer Schüttler (GER) 7-6 6-0 2-0 *(Schüttler
   retired)*

Ivo Karlovic (CRO) [14] beat Jan Minar (CZE) 7-5 6-1 6-4

James Blake (USA) [9] beat Donald Young (USA) 6-1 3-6 6-1

Steve Darcis (BEL) beat Denis Gremelmayr (GER) 6-1 6-7 7-6 6-4

Mardy Fish (USA) beat Robert Smeets (AUS) 7-6 6-7 6-3 6-4

Paul-Henri Mathieu [24] beat Sebastien Grosjean (FRA) 6-7 7-6 6-3 6-2

Gael Monfils (FRA) [32] beat Pablo Cuevas (URU) 6-4 6-4 6-1

Evgeny Korolev (KAZ) beat Robin Söderling (SWE) 7-6 6-3 7-6

Andrey Golubev (KAZ) beat Brendan Evans (USA) 6-4 6-3 6-2
David Nalbandian (ARG) beat Marcos Daniel (BRA) 6-1 6-2 6-4

David Ferrer (ESP) [4] beat Martin Vassallo Arguello (ARG) 7-6 6-2 6-2
Andreas Beck (GER) beat John Isner (USA) 7-6 6-4 7-6
Roko Karanusic (CRO) beat Ryan Sweeting (USA) 7-5 7-5 3-6 6-2
Kei Nishikori (JPN) beat Juan Monaco (ARG) [29] 6-2 6-2 5-7 6-2
Juan Martin Del Potro (ARG) [17] beat Guillermo Canas (ARG) 4-6 7-6
     6-4 6-1
Thomaz Bellucci (BRA) beat Oscar Hernandez (ESP) 6-3 6-7 6-4 7-5
Jose Acasuso (ARG) beat Michael Berrer (GER) 6-4 6-2 6-2
Gilles Simon (FRA) [16] beat Marcel Granollers (ESP) 6-4 6-3 5-7 6-2
Stanislav Wawrinka (SUI) [10] beat Simone Bolelli 7-6 6-3 6-3
Wayne Odesnik (USA) beat Fabio Fognini (ITA) 2-6 6-0 4-6 6-3 6-4
Lu Yen-hsun (TPE) beat Nicolas Lapentti (ECU) 6-4 1-6 4-6 6-4 6-3
Flavio Cipolla (ITA) beat Jan Hernych (CZE) 6-7 6-4 2-6 7-6 7-6
Jürgen Melzer (AUT) beat Feliciano Lopez (ESP) [27] 4-6 7-6 6-2 2-6 6-4
Jiri Vanek (CZE) beat Stephane Bohli (SUI) 3-6 6-3 6-2 7-5
Michael Llodra (FRA) beat Teymuraz Gabahvili (RUS) 6-3 5-7 7-6 7-6
Andy Murray (GBR) [6] beat Sergio Roitman (ARG) 6-3 6-4 6-0

Andy Roddick (USA) [8] beat Fabrice Santoro (FRA) 6-2 6-2 6-2
Ernests Gulbis (LAT) beat Thomas Johansson (SWE) 7-5 6-1 7-6
Guillermo Garcia Lopez (ESP) beat Dominik Hrbaty (SLO) 4-6 6-3 6-4 6-4
Andreas Seppi (ITA) [31] beat Lee Hyung-taik (KOR) 6-3 7-5 3-6 3-6 6-3
Ivo Minar (CZE) beat Nicolas Kiefer (GER) [20] 4-6 6-1 6-4 4-1 *(Kiefer*
     retired)
Jarkko Neiminen (FIN) beat Scoville Jenkins (USA) 6-3 6-3 7-5
Bobby Reynolds (USA) beat Tomas Zib (CZE) 6-4 6-7 2-6 6-4 7-6
Fernando Gonzalez (CHI) [11] beat Ivan Navarro (ESP) 7-6 6-3 4-6 7-6
Tommy Robredo (ESP) [15] beat Mischa Zverev (GER) 7-6 6-2 6-1
Marat Safin (RUS) beat Vincent Spadea (USA) 3-6 6-2 6-3 4-6 6-4
Carlos Moya (ESP) beat Aisam-ul-Haq Qureshi (PAK) 6-4 6-7 7-6 6-2

Jo-Wilfried Tsonga (FRA) [19] beat Santiago Ventura (ESP) 6-7 6-4 6-2 6-3
Marin Cilic (CRO) [30] beat Julien Benneteau (FRA) 4-6 7-5 6-3 6-7 6-2
Robby Ginepri (USA) beat Amer Delic (USA) 6-1 6-2 7-6
Robert Kendrick (USA) beat Nicolas Mahut (FRA) 7-6 6-4 5-7 7-5
Novak Djokovic (SRB) [3] beat Arnaud Clement (FRA) 6-3 6-3 6-4

Nikolay Davydenko (RUS) [5] beat Dudi Sela (ISR) 6-3 6-3 6-3
Agustin Calleri (ARG) beat Austin Krajicek (USA) 6-2 6-2 6-1
Victor Hanescu (ROU) beat Albert Montanes (ESP) 7-6 6-3 2-6 6-3
Dmitry Tursunov (RUS) [26] beat Eduardo Schwank (ARG) 7-5 4-6 7-5 7-6
Nicolas Almagro (ESP) [18] beat Frank Dancevic (CAN) 6-3 6-4 7-5
Sam Warburg (USA) beat Janko Tipsarevic (SRB) 6-2 1-0 *(Tipsarevic retired)*
Gilles Müller (LUX) beat Laurent Recouderc (FRA) 6-4 6-0 4-6 6-4
Tommy Haas (GER) beat Richard Gasquet (FRA) [12] 6-7 6-4 5-7 7-5 6-2
Fernando Verdasco (ESP) [13] beat Igor Kunitsyn (RUS) 6-3 6-4 6-1
Rui Machado (POR) beat Rik de Voest (ZA) 6-4 7-6 6-1
Jeremy Chardy (FRA) beat Frederico Gil (POR) 3-6 6-3 6-2 6-3
Igor Andreev (RUS) [23] beat Marc Gicquel (FRA) 7-6 6-4 6-4
Radek Stepanek (CZE) [28] beat Potito Starace (ITA) 7-5 6-3 6-1
Chris Guccione (AUS) beat Jesse Levine (USA) 6-3 3-6 7-6 7-6
Thiago Alves (BRA) beat Paul Capdeville (CHI) 4-6 1-6 6-1 7-6 6-4
Roger Federer (SUI) [2] beat Maximo Gonzalez (ARG) 6-3 6-0 6-3

Round 2

Rafa Nadal (ESP) [1] beat Ryler DeHeart (USA) 6-1 6-2 6-4
Viktor Troicki (SRB) beat Philipp Kohlschreiber (GER) [25] 2-6 6-3 6-4 3-0
   (Kohlschreiber retired)
Sam Querrey (USA) beat Nicolas Devilder (FRA) 7-6 6-4 4-6 6-3
Ivo Karlovic (CRO) [14] beat Florent Serra (FRA) 7-6 6-4 6-2
James Blake (USA) [9] beat Steve Darcis (BEL) 4-6 6-3 1-0 *(Darcis retired)*
Mardy Fish (USA) beat Paul-Henri Mathieu [24] 6-2 3-6 6-3 6-4
Gael Monfils (FRA) [32] beat Evgeny Korolev (KAZ) 6-2 6-3 3-6 6-4

David Nalbandian (ARG) beat Andrey Golubev (KAZ) 6-2 6-4 6-2

David Ferrer (ESP) [4] beat Andreas Beck (GER) 4-6 7-5 6-3 7-6

Kei Nishikori (JPN) beat Roko Karanusic (CRO) 6-1 7-5 *(Karanusic retired)*

Juan Martin Del Potro (ARG) [17] beat Thomaz Bellucci (BRA) 4-6 6-1 7-5 6-3

Gilles Simon (FRA) [16] beat Jose Acasuso (ARG) 6-4 6-1 6-4

Stanislav Wawrinka (SUI) [10] beat Wayne Odesnik (USA) 6-4 7-6 6-2

Flavio Cipolla (ITA) beat Lu Yen-hsun (TPE) 6-1 4-6 7-6 6-4

Jürgen Melzer (AUT) beat Jiri Vanek (CZE) 6-0 6-2 6-2

Andy Murray (GBR) [6] beat Michael Llodra (FRA) 6-7 4-6 7-6 6-1 6-3

Andy Roddick (USA) [8] beat Ernests Gulbis (LAT) 3-6 7-5 6-2 7-5

Andreas Seppi (ITA) [31] beat Guillermo Garcia Lopez (ESP) 6-2 4-6 6-2 6-2

Jarkko Neiminen (FIN) beat Ivo Minar (CZE) 6-7 3-6 6-4 6-3 6-2

Fernando Gonzalez (CHI) [11] beat Bobby Reynolds (USA) 7-6 6-4 6-4

Tommy Robredo (ESP) [15] beat Marat Safin (RUS) 4-6 7-6 6-4 6-0

Jo-Wilfried Tsonga (FRA) [19] beat Carlos Moya (ESP) 4-6 6-3 6-4 6-4

Marin Cilic (CRO) [30] beat Robby Ginepri (USA) 6-4 2-6 6-2 7-5

Novak Djokovic (SRB) [3] beat Robert Kendrick (USA) 7-6 6-4 6-4

Nikolay Davydenko (RUS) [5] beat Agustin Calleri (ARG) 6-4 6-4 7-6

Dmitry Tursunov (RUS) [26] beat Victor Hanescu (ROU) 6-7 6-3 6-4 6-2

Nicolas Almagro (ESP) [18] beat Sam Warburg (USA) 6-3 6-4 6-4

Gilles Müller (LUX) beat Tommy Haas (GER) 2-6 2-6 7-6 6-3 6-3

Fernando Verdasco (ESP) [13] beat Rui Machado (POR) 6-7 7-6 6-4 6-7 6-0

Igor Andreev (RUS) [23] beat Jeremy Chardy (FRA) 7-6 6-4 6-3

Radek Stepanek (CZE) [28] beat Chris Guccione (AUS) 6-4 6-4 6-7 6-2

Roger Federer (SUI) [2] beat Thiago Alves (BRA) 6-3 7-6 6-4

Round 3

Rafa Nadal (ESP) [1] beat Viktor Troicki (SRB) 6-4 6-3 6-0

Sam Querrey (USA) beat Ivo Karlovic (CRO) [14] 7-6 7-6 6-2

Mardy Fish (USA) beat James Blake (USA) [9] 6-3 6-3 7-6
Gael Monfils (FRA) [32] beat David Nalbandian (ARG) 6-3 6-4 6-2
Kei Nishikori (JPN) beat David Ferrer (ESP) [4] 6-4 6-4 3-6 2-6 7-5
Juan Martin Del Potro (ARG) [17] beat Gilles Simon (FRA) [16] 6-4 6-7
    6-1 3-6 6-3
Stanislav Wawrinka (SUI) [10] beat Flavio Cipolla (ITA) 5-7 6-7 6-4 6-0 6-4
Andy Murray (GBR) [6] beat Jürgen Melzer (AUT) 6-7 4-6 7-6 6-1
    6-3
Andy Roddick (USA) [8] beat Andreas Seppi (ITA) [31] 6-2 7-5 7-6
Fernando Gonzalez (CHI) [11] beat Jarkko Nieminen (FIN) 7-5 6-4 6-7
    6-1
Tommy Robredo (ESP) [15] beat Jo-Wilfried Tsonga (FRA) [19] 7-6 6-2
    6-3
Novak Djokovic (SRB) [3] beat Marin Cilic (CRO) [30] 6-7 7-5 6-4 7-6
Nikolay Davydenko (RUS) [5] beat Dmitry Tursunov (RUS) [26] 6-2 7-6
    6-3
Gilles Müller (LUX) beat Nicolas Almagro (ESP) [18] 6-7 3-6 7-6 7-6 7-5
Igor Andreev (RUS) [23] beat Fernando Verdasco (ESP) 6-2 6-4 6-4
Roger Federer (SUI) [2] beat Radek Stepanek (CZE) [28] 6-3 6-3 6-2

Round 4

Rafa Nadal (ESP) [1] beat Sam Querrey (USA) 6-2 5-7 7-6 6-3
Mardy Fish (USA) beat Gael Monfils (FRA) [32] 7-5 6-2 6-2
Juan Martin Del Potro (ARG) [17] beat Kei Nishikori (JPN) 6-3 6-4 6-3
Andy Murray (GBR) [6] beat Stanislav Wawrinka (SUI) [10] 6-1 6-3
    6-3
Andy Roddick (USA) [8] beat Fernando Gonzalez (CHI) [11] 6-2 6-4 6-1
Novak Djokovic (SRB) [3] beat Tommy Robredo (ESP) [15] 4-6 6-2 6-3
    5-7 6-3
Gilles Müller (LUX) beat Nikolay Davydenko (RUS) [5] 6-4 4-6 6-3 7-6
Roger Federer (SUI) [2] beat Igor Andreev (RUS) [23] 6-7 7-6 6-3 3-6 6-3

Quarter-finals

Rafa Nadal (ESP) [1] beat Mardy Fish (USA) 3-6 6-1 6-4 6-2

Andy Murray (GBR) [6] beat Juan Martin Del Potro (ARG) [17] 7-6 7-6 4-6 7-5

Novak Djokovic (SRB) [3] beat Andy Roddick (USA) [8] 6-2 6-3 3-6 7-6

Roger Federer (SUI) [2] beat Gilles Müller (LUX) 7-6 6-4 7-6

Semi-finals

Andy Murray (GBR) [6] beat Rafa Nadal (ESP) [1] 6-2 7-6 4-6 6-4

Roger Federer (SUI) [2] beat Novak Djokovic (SRB) [3] 6-3 5-7 7-5 6-2

Final

Roger Federer (SUI) [2] beat Andy Murray (GBR) [6] 6-2 7-5 6-2

US Open 2012

Round 1

Roger Federer (SWI) [1] beat Donald Young (USA) 6-3 6-2 6-4

Bjorn Phau (GER) beat Maxime Authom (BEL) 6-2 4-6 6-4 7-6

Albert Ramos (ESP) beat Robby Ginepri (USA) 6-7 7-5 6-4 6-0

Fernando Verdasco (ESP) [25] beat Rui Machado (POR) 6-1 6-2 6-4

Mardy Fish (USA) [23] beat Go Soeda (JPN) 7-6 7-6 6-3

Nikolay Davydenko (RUS) beat Guido Pella (ARG) 7-5 3-6 6-4 6-2

Jimmy Wang (TPE) beat Ivo Karlovic (CRO) 7-6 6-7 6-1 6-4

Gilles Simon (FRA) [16] beat Michael Russell (USA) 7-6 3-6 5-7 6-4 6-1

Nicolas Almagro (ESP) [11] beat Radek Stepanek (CZE) 6-4 6-7 6-3 6-4

Philipp Petzschner (GER) beat Nicolas Mahut (FRA) 1-6 4-6 6-4 7-5 7-6

Flavio Cipolla (ITA) beat Blaz Kavcic (SLO) 6-4 7-6 3-6 6-3

Jack Sock (USA) beat Florian Mayer (GER) [22] 6-3 6-2 3-2 *(Mayer retired)*

Sam Querrey (USA) [27] beat Yen-Hsun Lu (TPE) 6-7 6-4 6-4 7-5

Ruben Ramirez Hidalgo (ESP) beat Somdev Devvarman (IND) 6-3 6-2 3-6
   6-4

Jurgen Zopp (EST) beat Denis Istomin (UZB) 3-6 6-3 6-3 7-5
Tomas Berdych (CZE) [6] beat David Goffin (BEL) 7-5 6-3 6-3

Andy Murray (GBR) [3] beat Alex Bogomolov Jr. (RUS) 6-2 6-4 6-1
Ivan Dodig (CRO) beat Hiroki Moriya (JPN) 6-0 6-1 6-2
Pablo Andujar (ESP) beat Thomaz Bellucci (BRA) 7-6 (7-5) 3-6 7-6 7-5
Feliciano Lopez (ESP) [30] beat Robin Haase (NED) 6-3 7-5 6-2
Marcel Granollers (ESP) [24] beat Denis Kudla (USA) 6-3 4-6 6-3 7-6
James Blake (USA) beat Lukas Lacko (SVK) 7-5 6-2 3-6 6-3
Paul-Henri Mathieu (FRA) beat Igor Andreev (RUS) 2-6 4-6 7-6 7-6 6-1
Milos Raonic (CAN) [15] beat Santiago Giraldo (COL) 6-3 4-6 3-6 6-4 6-4
Marin Cilic (CRO) [12] beat Marinko Matosevic (AUS) 5-7 2-6 6-4 6-2 6-4
Daniel Brands (GER) beat Adrian Ungur (ROM) 7-6 6-4 7-6
Tim Smyczek (USA) beat Bobby Reynolds (USA) 1-6 6-4 6-2 4-6 6-4
Kei Nishikori (JPN) [17] beat Guido Andreozzi (ARG) 6-1 6-2 6-4
Jeremy Chardy (FRA) [32] beat Filippo Volandri (ITA) 6-3 6-4 6-3
Matthew Ebden (AUS) beat Tatsuma Ito (JPN) 7-6 6-3 6-2
Martin Klizan (SVK) beat Alejandro Falla (COL) 6-4 6-1 6-2
Jo-Wilfried Tsonga (FRA) [5] beat Karol Beck (SVK) 6-3 6-1 7-6

Janko Tipsarevic (SRB) [8] beat Guillaume Rufin (FRA) 4-6 3-6 6-2 6-3 6-2
Brian Baker (USA) beat Jan Hajek (Cze) 6-3 6-4 6-2
Grega Zemlja (SLO) beat Ricardo Mello (BRA) 7-5 7-6 7-5
Cedrik-Marcel Stebe (GER) beat Viktor Troicki (SRB) [29] 6-4 6-4 3-6 6-2
Philipp Kohlschreiber (GER) [19] beat Michael Llodra (FRA) 7-6 4-6 7-6
    6-1
Benoit Paire (FRA) beat Grigor Dimitrov (BUL) 5-7 6-3 7-6 6-2
Jarkko Nieminen (FIN) beat Mikhail Kukushkin (KAZ) 6-0 6-2 ret
John Isner (USA) [9] beat Xavier Malisse (BEL) 6-3 7-6 5-7 7-6
Richard Gasquet (FRA) [13] beat Albert Montanes (ESP) 4-6 6-2 6-3 6-3
Bradley Klahn (USA) beat Jurgen Melzer (AUT) 4-6 6-3 7-5 5-7 6-4
Steve Johnson (USA) beat Rajeev Ram (USA) 6-3 7-6 6-3
Ernests Gulbis (LAT) beat Tommy Haas (GER) [21] 3-6 4-6 6-4 7-5 6-3

Gilles Muller (LUX) beat Mikhail Youzhny (RUS) [28] 2-6 3-6 7-5 7-6 7-6
Lleyton Hewitt (AUS) beat Tobias Kamke (GER) 4-6 6-2 6-1 6-4
Igor Sijsling (NED) beat Daniel Gimeno-Traver (ESP) 7-5 6-3 6-4
David Ferrer (ESP) [4] beat Kevin Anderson (RSA) 6-4 6-2 7-6

Juan Martin Del Potro (ARG) [7] beat Florent Serra (FRA) 6-4 7-6 6-4
Ryan Harrison (USA) beat Benjamin Becker (GER) 7-5 6-4 6-2
Leonardo Mayer (ARG) beat Lukasz Kubot (POL) 6-4 6-4 7-5
Tommy Robredo (ESP) beat Andreas Seppi (ITA) [26] 6-1 7-5 6-3
Andy Roddick (USA) [20] beat Rhyne Williams (USA) 6-3 6-4 6-4
Bernard Tomic (AUS) beat Carlos Berlocq (ARG) 4-6 7-5 6-3 6-4
Fabio Fognini (ITA) beat Edouard Roger-Vasselin (FRA) 3-6 5-7 6-4 6-4
    7-5
Guillermo Garcia-Lopez (ESP) beat Juan Monaco (ARG) [10] 3-6 1-6 6-4
    7-6 7-6
Alexandr Dolgopolov (UKR) [14] beat Jesse Levine (USA) 3-6 4-6 6-4 6-1
    6-2
Marcos Baghdatis (CYP) beat Matthias Bachinger (GER) 6-2 4-6 6-4 6-7
    7-6
Steve Darcis (BEL) beat Malek Jaziri (TUN) 3-6 6-1 6-1 6-1
Stanislas Wawrinka (SWI) [18] beat Sergiy Stakhovsky (UKR) 6-7 7-6 6-4
    6-2
Julien Benneteau (FRA) [31] beat Olivier Rochus (BEL) 7-6 6-2 6-3
Dennis Novikov (USA) beat Jerzy Janowicz (POL) 6-2 7-6 3-6 6-3
Rogerio Dutra Silva (BRA) beat Teymuraz Gabashvili (RUS) 4-6 6-4 6-7 6-3
    7-5
Novak Djokovic (SRB) [2] beat Paolo Lorenzi (ITA) 6-1 6-0 6-1

Round 2

Roger Federer (SWI) [1] beat Bjorn Phau (GER) 6-2 6-3 6-2
Fernando Verdasco (ESP) [25] beat Albert Ramos (ESP) 7-6 5-7 7-6 6-4
Mardy Fish (USA) [23] beat Nikolay Davydenko (RUS) 4-6 6-7 6-2 6-1 6-2

Gilles Simon (FRA) [16] beat Jimmy Wang (TPE) 6-4 4-6 6-4 6-4

Nicolas Almagro (ESP) [11] beat Philipp Petzschner (GER) 6-3 5-7 5-7 6-4
6-4

Jack Sock (USA) beat Flavio Cipolla (ITA) 6-2 6-2 6-4

Sam Querrey (USA) [27] beat Ruben Ramirez Hidalgo (ESP) 6-3 6-4 6-3

Tomas Berdych (CZE) [6] beat Jurgen Zopp (EST) 6-1 6-4 6-2

Andy Murray (GBR) [3] beat Ivan Dodig (CRO) 6-2 6-1 6-3

Feliciano Lopez (ESP) [30] beat Pablo Andujar (ESP) 6-4 6-1 6-7 3-6 7-5

James Blake (USA) beat Marcel Granollers (ESP) [24] 6-1 6-4 6-2

Milos Raonic (CAN) [15] beat Paul-Henri Mathieu (FRA) 7-5 6-4 7-6

Marin Cilic (CRO) [12] beat Daniel Brands (GER) 6-3 6-2 5-7 4-6 7-5

Kei Nishikori (JPN) [17] beat Tim Smyczek (USA) 6-2 6-2 6-4

Jeremy Chardy (FRA) [32] beat Matthew Ebden (AUS) 6-4 6-2 6-2

Martin Klizan (SVK) beat Jo-Wilfried Tsonga (FRA) [5] 6-4 1-6 6-1 6-3

Janko Tipsarevic (SRB) [8] beat Brian Baker (USA) 6-4 6-3 6-4

Grega Zemlja (SLO) beat Cedrik-Marcel Stebe (GER) 6-4 2-6 6-4 6-4

Philipp Kohlschreiber (GER) [19] beat Benoit Paire (FRA) 6-7 6-3 3-6 6-2
7-6

John Isner (USA) [9] beat Jarkko Nieminen (FIN) 6-3 6-7 6-4 6-3

Richard Gasquet (FRA) [13] beat Bradley Klahn (USA) 6-3 6-3 6-1

Steve Johnson (USA) beat Ernests Gulbis (LAT) 6-7 7-6 6-3 6-4

Lleyton Hewitt (AUS) beat Gilles Muller (LUX) 3-6 7-6 6-7 7-5 6-4

David Ferrer (ESP) [4] beat Igor Sijsling (NED) 6-2 6-3 7-6

Juan Martin Del Potro (ARG) [7] beat Ryan Harrison (USA) 6-2 6-3 2-6 6-2

Leonardo Mayer (ARG) beat Tommy Robredo (ESP) 6-1 6-4 4-6 7-5

Andy Roddick (USA) [20] beat Bernard Tomic (AUS) 6-3 6-4 6-0

Fabio Fognini (ITA) beat Guillermo Garcia-Lopez (ESP) 6-4 6-4 6-2

Alexandr Dolgopolov (UKR) [14] beat Marcos Baghdatis (CYP) 6-4 3-6 6-0
7-6

Stanislas Wawrinka (SWI) [18] beat Steve Darcis (BEL) 6-7 6-3 4-6 6-1 7-5

Julien Benneteau (FRA) [31] beat Dennis Novikov (USA) 3-6 6-4 7-6 7-5

Novak Djokovic (SRB) [2] beat Rogerio Dutra Silva (BRA) 6-2 6-1 6-2

Round 3

Roger Federer (SWI) [1] beat Fernando Verdasco (ESP) [25] 6-3 6-4 6-4
Mardy Fish (USA) [23] beat Gilles Simon (FRA) [16] 6-1 5-7 7-6 6-3
Nicolas Almagro (ESP) [11] beat Jack Sock (USA) 7-6 6-7 7-6 6-1
Tomas Berdych (CZE) [6] beat Sam Querrey (USA) [27] 6-7 6-4 6-3 6-2
**Andy Murray (GBR) [3] beat Feliciano Lopez (ESP) [30] 7-6 7-6
4-6 7-6**
Milos Raonic (CAN) [15] beat James Blake (USA) 6-3 6-0 7-6
Marin Cilic (CRO) [12] beat Kei Nishikori (JPN) [17] 6-3 6-4 6-7 6-3
Martin Klizan (SVK) beat Jeremy Chardy (FRA) [32] 6-4 6-4 6-4
Janko Tipsarevic (SRB) [8] beat Grega Zemlja (SLO) 6-4 6-3 7-5
Philipp Kohlschreiber (GER) [19] beat John Isner (USA) [9] 6-4 3-6 4-6 6-3
6-4
Richard Gasquet (FRA) [13] beat Steve Johnson (USA) 7-6 6-2 6-3
David Ferrer (ESP) [4] beat Lleyton Hewitt (AUS) 7-6 4-6 6-3 6-0
Juan Martin Del Potro (ARG) [7] beat Leonardo Mayer (ARG) 6-3 7-5 7-6
Andy Roddick (USA) [20] beat Fabio Fognini (ITA) 7-5 7-6 4-6 6-4
Stanislas Wawrinka (SWI) [18] beat Alexandr Dolgopolov (UKR) [14]
Novak Djokovic (SRB) [2] beat Julien Benneteau (FRA) [31] 6-3 6-2 6-2

Round 4

Roger Federer (SWI) [1] w/o Mardy Fish (USA) [23]
Tomas Berdych (CZE) [6] beat Nicolas Almagro (ESP) [11] 7-6 6-4 6-1
Andy Murray (GBR) [3] beat Milos Raonic (CAN) [15] 6-4 6-4 6-2
Marin Cilic (CRO) [12] beat Martin Klizan (SVK) 7-5 6-4 6-0
Janko Tipsarevic (SRB) [8] beat Philipp Kohlschreiber (GER) [19] 6-3 7-6 6-2
David Ferrer (ESP) [4] beat Richard Gasquet (FRA) [13] 7-5 7-6 6-4
Juan Martin Del Potro (ARG) [7] beat Andy Roddick (USA) [20] 6-7 7-6
6-2 6-4
Novak Djokovic (SRB) [2] beat Stanislas Wawrinka (SWI) [18] 6-4 6-1 3-1
(Wawrinka retired)

Quarter-finals

Tomas Berdych (CZE) [6] beat Roger Federer (SWI) [1] 7-6 6-4 3-6 6-3

Andy Murray (GBR) [3] beat Marin Cilic (CRO) [12] 3-6 7-6 6-2 6-0

David Ferrer (ESP) [4] beat Janko Tipsarevic (SRB) [8] 6-3 6-7 2-6 6-3 7-6

Novak Djokovic (SRB) [2] beat Juan Martin Del Potro (ARG) [7] 6-2 7-6 6-4

Semi-finals

Andy Murray (GBR) [3] beat Tomas Berdych (CZE) [6] 5-7 6-2 6-1 7-6

Novak Djokovic (SRB) [2] beat David Ferrer (ESP) [4] 2-6 6-1 6-4 6-2

Final

Andy Murray (GBR) [3] beat Novak Djokovic (SRB) [2] 7-6 7-5 2-6 3-6 6-2

Wimbledon 2012

Round 1

Novak Djokovic (SRB) [1] beat Juan Carlos Ferrero 6-3 6-3 6-1

Ryan Harrison (USA) beat Yen-hsun Lu (TPE) 4-6 6-3 6-4 6-2

Benjamin Becker (GER) beat James Blake (USA) 6-7 7-5 6-0 6-4

Radek Stepanek (CZE) [28] beat Sergiy Stakhovsky (UKR) 6-1 1-0
  (Stakhovsky retired)

Viktor Troicki (SRB) beat Marcel Granollers (ESP) 7-5 7-6 3-6 2-6 8-6

Martin Klizan (SVK) beat Juan Ignacio Chela (ARG) 7-5 3-6 7-6 1-6 11-9

Jeremy Chardy (FRA) beat Filippo Volandri (ITA) 6-0 6-1 1-0 *(Volandri
  retired)*

Juan Monaco (ARG) [15] beat Leonardo Mayer ARG 6-4 7-6 7-6

Nicolas Almagro (ESP) [12] beat Olivier Rochus (BEL) 6-7 3-6 7-6 6-2 6-4

Guilaume Rufin (FRA) beat Steve Darcis (BEL) 6-4 3-6 5-7 6-4 6-4

Ruben Bemelmans (BEL) beat Carlos Berlocq (ARG) 7-5 6-7 6-3 7-6

Richard Gasquet (FRA) [18] beat Tobias Kamke (GER) 6-2 6-2 6-2

Florian Mayer (GER) [31] beat Dmitry Tursunov (RUS) 7-6 6-2 6-3

Philipp Petzchner (GER) beat Blaz Kavcic (SLO) 6-4 6-4 6-2
Jerzy Janowicz (POL) beat Simone Bolelli (ITA) 3-6 6-3 6-3 6-3
Ernests Gulbis (LAT) beat Tomas Berdych (CZE) [6] 7-6 7-6 7-6

Roger Federer (SUI) [3] beat Albert Ramos (ESP) 6-1 6-1 6-1
Fabio Fognini (ITA) beat Michael Llodra (FRA) 3-6 6-3 6-4 7-5
Michael Russell (USA) beat Adrian Menendez-MacEiras (ESP) 6-3 6-1 7-6
Julien Benneteau (FRA) [29] beat Gilles Muller (LUX) 6-2 7-5 7-6
Fernando Verdasco (ESP) [17] beat Jimmy Wang (TPE) 7-6 6-4 7-5
Grega Zemlja (SLO) beat Josh Goodall (GBR) 6-4 3-6 7-6 6-4
Xavier Malisse (BEL) beat Marinko Matosevic (AUS) 6-2 6-2 7-5
Gilles Simon (FRA) [13] beat Paul-Henri Mathieu (FRA) 6-3 5-4 *(Mathieu retired)*
Alejandro Falla (COL) beat John Isner (USA) [11] 6-4 6-7 3-6 7-6 7-5
Nicolas Mahut (FRA) beat Paolo Lorenzi (ITA) 6-3 5-7 6-7 7-5 6-2
Igor Andreev (RUS) beat Oliver Golding (GBR) 6-1 7-6 7-6 7-5
Denis Istomin (UZB) beat Andreas Seppi (ITA) 6-7 6-4 3-6 6-3 8-6
Mikhail Youzhny (RUS) [26] beat Donald Young (USA) 4-6 6-3 6-2 6-3
Inigo Cervantes (ESP) beat Flavio Cipolla (ITA) 2-6 6-7 6-3 6-2 6-1
Ryan Sweeting (USA) beat Potito Starace (ITA) 6-2 2-0 *(Starace retired)*
Janko Tipsarevic (SRB) [8] beat David Nalbandian (ARG) 6-4 7-6 6-2

David Ferrer (ESP) [7] beat Dustin Brown GER 7-6 6-4 6-4
Kenny De Schepper (FRA) beat Matthias Bachinger (GER) 6-4 6-2 6-2
Bjorn Phau (GER) beat Wayne Odesnik (USA) 6-3 3-6 7-6 3-6 4-6
Andy Roddick (USA) beat Jamie Baker (GBR) 7-6 6-4 7-5
Kei Nishikori (JPN) [19] beat Mikhail Kukushkin (KAZ) 7-6 6-3 6-4
Florent Serra (FRA) beat Andrey Kuznetsov (RUS) 3-6 7-6 6-4 4-6 6-4
Go Soeda (JPN) beat Igor Kunitsyn (RUS) 6-3 6-2 6-1
Juan Martin Del Potro (ARG) [9] beat Robin Haase (NED) 6-4 3-6 7-6 7-5
Marin Cilic (CRO) [16] beat Cedrik-Marcel Stebe (GER) 6-4 3-6 6-3 6-2
Lukasz Kubot (POL) beat Tatsuma (JPN) 7-6 6-3 6-3
Sam Querrey (USA) beat Vasek Pospisil (CAN) 7-5 6-7 6-3 6-4

Milos Raonic (CAN) [21] beat Santiago Giraldo (COL) 6-4 6-4 6-4
Grigor Dimitrov (BUL) beat Kevin Anderson (RSA) 7-5 7-6 6-7 6-3
Marcos Baghdatis (CYP) beat Albert Montanes (ESP) 6-2 6-4 6-4
Ivo Karlovic (CRO) beat Dudi Sela (ISR) 6-4 6-4 7-6
Andy Murray (GBR) [4] beat Nikolay Davydenko (RUS) 6-1 6-1 6-4

Jo-Wilfried Tsonga (FRA) [5] beat Lleyton Hewitt (AUS) 6-3 6-4 6-4
Guillermo Garcia-Lopez (ESP) beat Edouard Roger Vasselin (FRA) 6-7 6-3
    7-6 5-7 10-8
Lukas Lacko (SVK) beat Adrian Ungur (ROU) 7-6 6-1 6-3
Jürgen Melzer (AUT) beat Stanislav Wawrinka (SUI) [25] 3-6 7-6 2-6 6-4
    8-6
David Goffin (BEL) beat Bernard Tomic (AUS) [20] 3-6 6-3 6-4 6-4
Jesse Levine (USA) beat Karol Beck (SVK) 6-4 6-7 6-3 6-2
James Ward (GBR) beat Pablo Andujar (ESP) 4-6 6-0 3-6 6-3 6-3
Mardy Fish (USA) beat Ruben Ramirez Hidalgo (ESP) 7-6 7-5 7-5
Jarkko Nieminen (FIN) beat Feliciano Lopez (ESP) [14] 7-6 3-6 7-6 6-4
Brian Baker (USA) beat Rui Machado (POR) 7-6 6-4 6-0
Benoit Paire (FRA) beat Matthew Ebden (AUS) 6-1 6-3 6-7 6-3
Alexandr Dolgopolov (UKR) [22] beat Alex Bogomolov Jr. (RUS) 6-3 6-4
    7-5
Philipp Kohlschreiber (GER) [27] beat Tommy Haas (GER) 3-6 7-6 6-7 7-6
    6-2
Malek Jaziri (TUN) beat Jurgen Zopp (EST) 4-6 4-6 6-3 6-4 9-7
Lukas Rosol (CZE) beat Ivan Dodig (CRO) 6-4 3-6 7-6 7-5
Rafael Nadal (ESP) [2] beat Thomaz Bellucci (BRA) 7-6 6-2 6-3

Round 2

Novak Djokovic (SRB) [1] beat Ryan Harrison (USA) 6-4 6-4 6-4
Radek Stepanek (CZE) [28] beat Benjamin Becker (GER) 6-2 7-6 6-3
Viktor Troicki (SRB) beat Martin Klizan (SVK) 6-4 4-6 5-7 7-6 6-4
Juan Monaco (ARG) [15] beat Jeremy Chardy (FRA) 6-2 3-6 6-3 7-6

Nicolas Almagro (ESP) [12] beat Guilaume Rufin (FRA) 6-2 5-7 6-2 6-4

Richard Gasquet (FRA) [18] beat Ruben Bemelmans (BEL) 6-3 6-4 6-4

Florian Mayer (GER) [31] beat Philipp Petzchner (GER) 3-6 3-6 6-4 6-2 6-4

Jerzy Janowicz (POL) beat Ernests Gulbis (LAT) 2-6 6-4 3-6 7-6 9-7

Roger Federer (SUI) [3] beat Fabio Fognini (ITA) 6-1 6-3 6-2

Julien Benneteau (FRA) [29] beat Michael Russell (USA) 7-6 2-6 6-4 7-5

Fernando Verdasco (ESP) [17] beat Grega Zemlja (SLO) 7-6 7-6 3-6 6-3

Xavier Malisse (BEL) beat Gilles Simon (FRA) [13] 6-4 6-4 7-6

Alejandro Falla (COL) beat Nicolas Mahut (FRA) 6-4 6-3 4-6 4-6 7-5

Denis Istomin (UZB) beat Igor Andreev (RUS) 6-3 7-6 4-6 6-2

Mikhail Youzhny (RUS) [26] beat Inigo Cervantes (ESP) 6-1 6-3 6-4

Janko Tipsarevic (SRB) [8] beat Ryan Sweeting (USA) 5-7 7-5 6-4 6-2

David Ferrer (ESP) [7] beat Kenny De Schepper (FRA) 7-6 6-2 6-4

Andy Roddick (USA) beat Bjorn Phau (GER) 6-3 7-6 6-3

Kei Nishikori (JPN) [19] beat Florent Serra (FRA) 6-3 7-5 6-2

Juan Martin Del Potro (ARG) [9] beat Go Soeda (JPN) 6-2 6-3 1-6 6-4

Marin Cilic (CRO) [16] beat Lukasz Kubot (POL) 7-6 6-2 6-1

Sam Querrey (USA) beat Milos Raonic (CAN) [21] 6-7 7-6 7-6 6-4

Marcos Baghdatis (CYP) beat Grigor Dimitrov (BUL) 7-5 4-1 *(Dimitrov retired)*

Andy Murray (GBR) [4] beat Ivo Karlovic (CRO) 7-5 6-7 6-2 7-6

Jo-Wilfried Tsonga (FRA) [5] beat Guillermo Garcia-Lopez (ESP) 6-7 6-4 6- 6-3

Lukas Lacko (SVK) beat Jürgen Melzer (AUT) 6-4 6-7 3-6 6-3 6-4

David Goffin (BEL) beat Jesse Levine (USA) 4-6 6-4 6-1 6-3

Mardy Fish (USA) beat James Ward (GBR) 6-3 5-7 6-4 6-7 6-3

Brian Baker (USA) beat Jarkko Nieminen (FIN) 6-0 6-2 6-4

Benoit Paire (FRA) beat Alexandr Dolgopolov (UKR) [22] 7-6 6-4 6-4

Philipp Kohlschreiber (GER) [27] beat Malek Jaziri (TUN) 6-1 7-6 6-1

Lukas Rosol (CZE) beat Rafael Nadal (ESP) [2] 6-7 6-4 6-4 2-6 6-4

Round 3

Novak Djokovic (SRB) [1] beat Radek Stepanek (CZE) [28] 4-6 6-2 6-2 6-2

Viktor Troicki (SRB) beat Juan Monaco (ARG) [15] 7-5 7-5 6-3

Richard Gasquet (FRA) [18] beat Nicolas Almagro (ESP) [12] 6-3 6-4 6-4

Florian Mayer (GER) [31] beat Jerzy Janowicz (POL) 7-6 3-6 2-6 6-3 7-5

Roger Federer (SUI) [3] beat Julien Benneteau (FRA) [29] 4-6 6-7 6-2 7-6 6-1

Xavier Malisse (BEL) beat Fernando Verdasco (ESP) [17] 1-6 7-6 6-1 4-6 6-3

Denis Istomin (UZB) beat Alejandro Falla (COL) 6-3 6-4 3-6 7-6

Mikhail Youzhny (RUS) [26] beat Janko Tipsarevic (SRB) [8] 6-3 6-4 3-6 6-3

David Ferrer (ESP) [7] beat Andy Roddick (USA) 2-6 7-6 6-4 6-3

Juan Martin Del Potro (ARG) [9] beat Kei Nishikori (JPN) [19] 6-3 7-6 6-1

Marin Cilic (CRO) [16] beat Sam Querrey (USA) 7-6 6-4 6-2 6-7 17-15

Andy Murray (GBR) [4] beat Marcos Baghdatis (CYP) 7-5 3-6 7-5 6-1

Jo-Wilfried Tsonga (FRA) [5] beat Lukas Lacko (SVK) 6-4 6-3 6-3

Mardy Fish (USA) beat David Goffin (BEL) 6-3 7-6 7-6

Brian Baker (USA) beat Benoit Paire (FRA) 6-4 4-6 6-1 6-3

Philipp Kohlschreiber (GER) [27] beat Lukas Rosol (CZE) 6-2 6-3 7-6

Round 4

Novak Djokovic (SRB) [1] beat Viktor Troicki (SRB) 6-3 6-1 6-3

Florian Mayer (GER) [31] beat Richard Gasquet (FRA) [18] 6-3 6-1 3-6 6-2

Roger Federer (SUI) [3] beat Xavier Malisse (BEL) 7-6 6-1 4-6 6-3

Mikhail Youzhny (RUS) [26] beat Denis Istomin (UZB) 6-3 5-7 6-4 6-7 7-5

David Ferrer (ESP) [7] beat Juan Martin Del Potro (ARG) [9] 6-3 6-2 6-3

Andy Murray (GBR) [4] beat Marin Cilic (CRO) [16] 7-5 6-2 6-3

Jo-Wilfried Tsonga (FRA) [5] beat Mardy Fish (USA) 4-6 7-6 6-4 6-4

Philipp Kohlschreiber (GER) [27] beat Brian Baker (USA) 6-1 7-6 6-3

Quarter-finals

Novak Djokovic (SRB) [1] beat Florian Mayer (GER) [31] 6-4 6-1 6-4

Roger Federer (SUI) [3] beat Mikhail Youzhny (RUS) [26] 6-1 6-2 6-2

Andy Murray (GBR) [4] beat David Ferrer (ESP) [7] 6-7 7-6 6-4 7-6

Jo-Wilfried Tsonga (FRA) [5] beat Philipp Kohlschreiber (GER) [27]

Semi-finals

Roger Federer (SUI) [3] beat Novak Djokovic (SRB) [1] 6-3 3-6 6-4 6-3

Andy Murray (GBR) [4] beat Jo-Wilfried Tsonga (FRA) [5] 6-3 6-4 3-6 7-5

Final

Roger Federer (SUI) [3] beat Andy Murray (GBR) [4] 4-6 7-5 6-3 6-4

Wimbledon 2013

Round 1

Novak Djokovic (SRB) [1] beat Florian Mayer (GER) 6-3 7-5 6-4

Bobby Reynolds (USA) beat Steve Johnson (USA) 1-6 7-6 6-3 6-7 6-4

Jan-Lennard Struff (GER) beat Blaz Kavcic (SLO) 6-4 6-1 6-3

Jeremy Chardy (FRA) [28] beat Ryan Harrison 7-6 4-6 7-5 6-2

Feliciano Lopez (ESP) beat Gilles Simon [19] 6-2 6-4 7-6

Paul-Henri Mathieu (FRA) beat Ricardas Berankis (LTU) 7-6 7-5 6-7 6-4

Jimmy Wang (TPE) beat Wayne Odesnik (USA) 7-6 4-6 6-2 3-6 7-5

Tommy Haas (GER) beat Dmitry Tursunov (RUS) 6-3 7-5 7-5

Richard Gasquet (FRA) [9] beat Marcel Granollers (ESP) 6-7 6-4 7-5 6-4

Go Soeda (JPN) beat Andreas Haider- Maurer (AUT) 7-6 7-5 6-1

James Blake (USA) beat Thiemo De Bakker (NED) 6-1 6-3 6-2

Bernard Tomic (AUS) beat Sam Querrey (USA) [21] 7-6 7-6 3-6 2-6 6-3

Kevin Anderson (RSA) [27] beat Olivier Rochus (BEL) 6-4 6-2 6-1

Michal Przysiezny (POL) beat Philipp Petzschner (GER) 6-3 7-6 6-0

Daniel Brands (GER) beat Daniel Gimeno-Traver (ESP) 7-6 6-7 6-7 6-1 6-4

Tomas Berdych (CZE) [7] beat Martin Klizan (SVK) 6-3 6-4 6-4

David Ferrer (ESP) [4] beat Martin Alund (ARG) 6-1 4-6 7-5 6-2

Roberto Bautista Agut (ESP) beat Teymuraz Gabashvili (RUS) 6-3 6-4 7-6

Santiago Giraldo (COL) beat Horacio Zeballos (ARG) 3-6 7-6 6-7 6-1 6-3

Alexandr Dolgopolov (UKR) beat Gastao Elias (POR) 6-1 7-6 6-2

Milos Raonic (CAN) [17] beat Carlos Berlocq (ARG) 6-4 6-3 6-3

Igor Sijsling (NED) beat Alex Kuznetsov (USA) 6-3 6-4 6-4

Denis Judia (USA) beat James Duckworth (AUS) 6-4 6-2 3-6 4-6 6-1

Ivan Dodig (CRO) beat Philipp Kohlschreiber (GER) [16] 4-6 6-7 7-6 6-3
2-1 *(Kohlschreiber retired)*

Kei Nishikori (JPN) [12] beat Matthew Ebden (AUS) 6-2 6-4 6-3

Leonardo Mayer (ARG) beat Aljaz Bedene (SLO) 6-2 6-3 6-4

Michael Llodra (FRA) beat Jarkko Niemenen (FIN) 7-6 6-4 6-3

Andreas Seppi (ITA) [23] beat Denis Istomin (UZB) 7-6 7-6 5-7 3-6 6-3

Grigor Dimitrov (BUL) [29] beat Simone Bolelli (ITA) 6-1 6-4 6-3

Grega Zemlja (SLO) beat Michael Russell (USA) 6-7 6-4 6-4 6-1

Jesse Levine (CAN) beat Guido Pella (ARG) 6-4 6-2 4-6 3-6 4-3 *(Pella retired)*

Juan Martin Del Potro (ARG) [8] beat Albert Ramos (ESP) 6-2 7-5 6-1

Steve Darcis (BEL) beat Rafael Nadal (ESP) [5] 7-6 7-6 6-4

Lukasz Kubot (POL) beat Igor Andreev (RUS) 6-1 7-5 6-2

Stephane Robert (FRA) beat Alejandro Falla (COL) 6-3 7-6 7-5

Benoit Paire (FRA) [25] beat Adrian Ungur (ROU) beat 6-4 4-6 6-3 6-1

John Isner (USA) [18] beat Evgeny Donskoy (RUS) 6-1 7-6 7-6

Adrian Mannarino (FRA) beat Pablo Andujar (ESP) 6-1 6-2 6-3

Dustin Brown (GER) beat Guillermo Garcia-Lopez (ESP) 6-3 6-3 6-3

Lleyton Hewitt (AUS) beat Stanislas Wawrinka (SUI) [11] 6-4 7-5 6-3

Nicolas Almagro (ESP) [15] beat Jurgen Zopp (EST) 6-4 7-6 7-5

Guillaume Rufin (FRA) beat Marinko Matosevic (AUS) 6-1 4-6 6-4 6-3

Radek Stepanek (CZE) beat Matt Reid (AUS) 6-2 6-2 6-4

Jerzy Janowicz (POL) [24] beat Kyle Edmund (GBR) 6-2 6-2 6-4

Jürgen Melzer (AUT) beat Fabio Fognini (ITA) [30] 6-7 7-5 6-3 6-2

Julian Reister (GER) beat Lukas Rosol (CZE) 6-3 4-6 7-6 6-7 6-4

Sergiy Stakhovsky (UKR) beat Rogerio Dutra Silva (BRA) 6-4 6-0 6-4
Roger Federer (SUI) [3] beat Victor Hanescu (ROU) 6-3 6-2 6-0

Jo-Wilfried Tsonga (FRA) [6] beat David Goffin (BEL) 7-6 6-4 6-3
Ernests Gulbis (LAT) beat Edouard Roger Vasselin (FRA) 7-6 6-4 7-5
Fernando Verdasco (ESP) beat Xavier Malisse (BEL) 6-7 6-1 6-4 6-3
Julien Benneteau (FRA) beat Tobias Kamke (GER) 6-4 6-7 6-4 6-2
Juan Monaco (ARG) [22] beat Bastian Knittel (GER) 6-4 6-2 6-3
Rajeev Ram (USA) beat Lukas Lacko (SVK) 7-6 6-4 6-7 6-2
Kenny De Schepper (FRA) beat Paolo Lorenzi (ITA) 7-6 6-4 6-2
Marin Cilic (CRO) [10] beat Marcos Baghdatis (CYP) 6-3 6-4 6-4
Victor Troicki (SRB) beat Janko Tipsarevic (SRB) [14] 6-3 6-4 7-6
Andrey Kuznetsov (RUS) beat Albert Montanes (ESP) 6-3 6-4 3-6 6-3
Vasek Popspisil (CAN) beat Marc Gicquel (FRA) 6-3 6-2 7-6
Mikhail Youzhny (RUS) beat Robin Haase (NED) 6-4 7-5 7-5
Tommy Robredo (ESP) [32] beat Alex Bogomolov Jr. (RUS) 6-2 6-2 6-4
Nicolas Mahut (FRA) beat Jan Hajek (CZE) 6-2 6-4 6-3
Yen-hsun Lu (TPE) beat James Ward (GBR) 6-7 6-4 7-6 7-6
Andy Murray (GBR) [2] beat Benjamin Becker (GER) 6-4 6-3 6-2

Round 2

Novak Djokovic (SRB) [1] beat Bobby Reynolds (USA) 7-6 6-3 6-1
Jeremy Chardy (FRA) [28] beat Jan-Lennard Struff (GER) 6-2 5-7 7-6 7-6
Feliciano Lopez (ESP) beat Paul-Henri Mathieu (FRA) 6-3 5-1 *(Mathieu retired)*
Tommy Haas (GER) [13] beat Jimmy Wang (TPE) 6-3 6-2 7-5
Richard Gasquet (FRA) [9] beat Go Soeda (JPN) 6-0 6-3 6-7 7-6
Bernard Tomic (AUS) beat James Blake (USA) 6-3 6-4 7-5
Kevin Anderson (RSA) [27] beat Michal Przysiezny (POL) 6-4 7-6 6-4
Tomas Berdych (CZE) [7] beat Daniel Brands (GER) 7-6 6-4 6-2
David Ferrer (ESP) [4] beat Roberto Bautista Agut (ESP) 6-3 3-6 7-6 7-5
Alexandr Dolgopolov (UKR) beat Santiago Giraldo (COL) 6-4 7-5 6-3

Igor Sijsling (NED) beat Milos Raonic (CAN) [17] 7-5 6-4 7-6
Ivan Dodig (CRO) beat Denis Judia (USA) 6-1 7-6 7-5
Kei Nishikori (JPN) [12] beat Leonardo Mayer (ARG) 7-6 6-4 6-2
Andreas Seppi (ITA) [23] beat Michael Llodra (FRA) 7-5 *(Llodra retired)*
Grega Zemlja (SLO) beat Grigor Dimitrov (BUL) [29] 3-6 7-6 3-6 6-4 11-9
Juan Martin Del Potro (ARG) [8] beat Jesse Levine (CAN) 6-2 7-6 6-3

Lukasz Kubot (POL) w/o Steve Darcis (BEL)
Benoit Paire (FRA) [25] beat Stephane Robert (FRA) 6-4 7-5 6-4
Adrian Mannarino (FRA) beat John Isner (USA) [18] 1-1 *(Isner retired)*
Dustin Brown (GER) beat Lleyton Hewitt (AUS) 6-4 6-4 6-7 6-2
Nicolas Almagro (ESP) [15] beat Guillaume Rufin (FRA) 7-5 6-7 6-3 6-4
Jerzy Janowicz (POL) [24] beat Radek Stepanek (CZE) 6-2 5-3 *(Stepanek retired)*
Jürgen Melzer (AUT) beat Julian Reister (GER) 3-6 7-6 7-6 6-2
Sergiy Stakhovsky (UKR) beat Roger Federer (SUI) [3] 6-7 7-6 7-5 7-6
Ernests Gulbis (LAT) beat Jo-Wilfried Tsonga (FRA) [6] 3-6 6-3 6-3 *(Tsonga retired)*
Fernando Verdasco (ESP) beat Julien Benneteau (FRA) 7-6 7-6 6-4
Juan Monaco (ARG) [22] beat Rajeev Ram (USA) 5-7 6-2 6-4 6-2
Kenny De Schepper (FRA) w/o Marin Cilic (CRO) [10]
Victor Troicki (SRB) beat Andrey Kuznetsov (RUS) 6-4 6-3 6-4
Mikhail Youzhny (RUS) beat Vasek Popspisil (CAN) 6-2 6-7 7-6 3-6 6-4
Tommy Robredo (ESP) [32] beat Nicolas Mahut (FRA) 7-6 6-1 7-6
Andy Murray (GBR) [2] beat Yen-hsun Lu (TPE) 6-3 6-3 7-5

Round 3

Novak Djokovic (SRB) [1] beat Jeremy Chardy (FRA) [28] 6-3 6-2 6-2
Tommy Haas (GER) [13] beat Feliciano Lopez (ESP) 4-6 6-2 7-5 6-4
Bernard Tomic (AUS) beat Richard Gasquet (FRA) [9] 7-6 5-7 7-5 7-6
Tomas Berdych (CZE) [7] beat Kevin Anderson (RSA) [27] 3-6 6-3 6-4 7-5
David Ferrer (ESP) [4] beat Alexandr Dolgopolov (UKR) 6-7 7-6 2-6 6-1
   6-2

Ivan Dodig (CRO) beat Igor Sijsling (NED) 6-0 6-1 1-0 *(Sijsling retired)*

Andreas Seppi (ITA) [23] beat Kei Nishikori (JPN) [12] 3-6 6-2 6-7 6-1 6-4

Juan Martin Del Potro (ARG) [8] beat Grega Zemlja (SLO) 7-5 7-6 6-0

Lukasz Kubot (POL) beat Benoit Paire (FRA) [25] 6-1 6-3 6-4

Adrian Mannarino (FRA) beat Dustin Brown (GER) 6-4 6-2 7-5

Jerzy Janowicz (POL) [24] beat Nicolas Almagro (ESP) [15] 7-6 6-3 6-4

Jürgen Melzer (AUT) beat Sergiy Stakhovsky (UKR) 6-2 2-6 7-5 6-3

Fernando Verdasco (ESP) beat Ernests Gulbis (LAT) 6-2 6-4 6-4

Kenny De Schepper (FRA) beat Juan Monaco (ARG) [22] 6-4 7-6 6-4

Mikhail Youzhny (RUS) beat Victor Troicki (SRB) 6-3 6-4 7-5

Andy Murray (GBR) [2] beat Tommy Robredo (ESP) [32] 6-2 6-4 7-5

Round 4

Novak Djokovic (SRB) [1] beat Tommy Haas (GER) [13] 6-1 6-4 7-5

Tomas Berdych (CZE) [7] beat Bernard Tomic (AUS) 7-6 6-7 6-4 6-4

David Ferrer (ESP) [4] beat Ivan Dodig (CRO) 6-7 7-6 6-1 6-1

Juan Martin Del Potro (ARG) [8] beat Andreas Seppi (ITA) [23] 6-4 7-6 6-3

Lukasz Kubot (POL) beat Adrian Mannarino (FRA) 4-6 6-3 3-6 6-3 6-4

Jerzy Janowicz (POL) [24] beat Jürgen Melzer (AUT) 3-6 7-6 6-4 4-6 6-4

Fernando Verdasco (ESP) beat Kenny De Schepper (FRA) 6-4 6-4 6-4

Andy Murray (GBR) [2] beat Mikhail Youzhny (RUS) 6-4 7-6 6-1

Quarter-finals

Novak Djokovic (SRB) [1] beat Tomas Berdych (CZE) [7] 7-6 6-4 6-3

Juan Martin Del Potro (ARG) [8] beat David Ferrer (ESP) [4] 6-2 6-4 7-6

Jerzy Janowicz (POL) [24] beat Lukasz Kubot (POL) 7-5 6-4 6-4

Andy Murray (GBR) [2] beat Fernando Verdasco (ESP) 4-6 3-6 6-1 6-4 7-5

Semi-finals

Novak Djokovic (SRB) [1] beat Juan Martin Del Potro (ARG) [8] 7-5 4-6
7-6 6-7 6-3

**Andy Murray (GBR) [2] beat Jerzy Janowicz (POL) [24] 6-7 6-4 6-4
6-3**

Final

Andy Murray (GBR) [2] beat Novak Djokovic (SRB) [1] 6-4 7-6 6-4

Sources:
www.wimbledon.com
www.ausopen.com
www.usopen.org
www.dailymail.co.uk
www.wikipedia.org

Picture Credits

Section 1

1: Colorsport/Andrew Cowie; 2 (top & bottom): Colorsport/Andrew Cowie; 3: Getty Images/Julian Finney; 4 (top): Colorsport/Andrew Cowie; 4 (bottom): Getty Images/Chris McGrath; 5 (top): Getty Images/Bloomberg; 5 (bottom) Fotosports International/Tim Parker; 6: Action Images/Tony O'Brien/Livepic; 7 (top): Dave Shopland; 7 (bottom left): Getty Images/Clive Brunskill; 7 (bottom right): Offside/L'Equipe; 8 (top left): Action Images/Reuters/Aly Song; 8 (top right): Getty Images/Bradley Kanaris; 8 (centre right): Getty Images/Matthew Stockman; 8 (bottom): Action Images/Reuters/Steve Crisp

Section 2

9: Getty Images/Clive Brunskill; 10 (top & bottom): Dave Shopland; 11 (top): Getty Images/Clive Brunskill; 11 (bottom): Getty Images/Jeff J. Mitchell; 12 (top): Getty Images/Clive Brunskill; 12 (bottom): Fotosports International/Dan Beineke; 13 (top): Press Association Images/Jonathan Brady/PA Wire; 13 (bottom): Corbis/EPA/Anja Niedringhaus; 14, 15 (top): Getty Images/Julian Finney; 15 (bottom left): Offside/L'Equipe; 15 (bottom right): Action Images/Wang Lili/Xinhua/ZUMAPRESS.com; 16 (top): Action Images/Reuters/Suzanne Plunkett; 16 (bottom): Colorsport/Andrew Cowie